FORM AND TRANSFORMATION
A Study in the Philosophy of Plotinus

Plotinus, the father of Neoplatonism, lived in Rome during the third century A.D. As the last great philosopher in the ancient Greek tradition, he is a figure of commanding importance. Despite a marked increase in Plotinus scholarship since the 1970's, the need has been felt for a book to make Plotinus more generally accessible.

The role of the Form as an intrinsically valuable object of intellective and spiritual vision is often marginalized by the concern in contemporary Plato scholarship for its function as cause in ontology, epistemology, and ethics. Schroeder argues that the intrinsic value of Form is central to Plotinus' thought. It is indeed an object of ecstatic contemplation. Yet Plotinus builds its intrinsic value into the very structure of his understanding of creation in such a way that its philosophical uses need not be considered in abstraction from our enjoyment of it.

The author initiates us into Plotinus' thought by a deft exploration of the themes of form, light, silence, language, and love, and the vocabulary that weaves these together in such a way that the reader is enabled to begin reading Plotinus with understanding. Schroeder displays, as well as demonstrates discursively, what Plotinus understood by his doctrine of the sovereignty of Form.

FREDERIC M. SCHROEDER is an associate professor in the Department of Classics, Queen's University.

McGill-Queen's Studies in the History of Ideas

1 Problems of Cartesianism
Edited by Thomas M. Lennon, John M. Nicholas, and
John W. Davis

2 The Development of the Idea of History in Antiquity
Gerald A. Press

3 Claude Buffier and Thomas Reid:
Two Common-Sense Philosophers
Louise Marcil-Lacoste

4 Schiller, Hegel, and Marx:
State, Society, and the Aesthetic Ideal of Ancient Greece
Philip J. Kain

5 John Case and Aristotelianism in Renaissance England
Charles B. Schmitt

6 Beyond Liberty and Property:
The Process of Self-Recognition in Eighteenth-Century
Political Thought
J.A.W. Gunn

7 John Toland: His Methods, Manners, and Mind
Stephen H. Daniel

8 Coleridge and the Inspired Word
Anthony John Harding

9 The Jena System, 1804–5: Logic and Metaphysics
G.W.F. Hegel
Translation edited by John W. Burbidge and George di Giovanni
Introduction and notes by H.S. Harris

10 Consent, Coercion, and Limit:
The Medieval Origins of Parliamentary Democracy
Arthur P. Monahan

11 Scottish Common Sense in Germany, 1768–1800:
A Contribution to the History of Critical Philosophy
Manfred Kuehn

12 Paine and Cobbett:
The Transatlantic Connection
David A. Wilson

13 Descartes and the Enlightenment
Peter A. Schouls

14 Greek Scepticism
Anti-Realist Trends in Ancient Thought
Leo Groarke

15 The Irony of Theology and the Nature of Religious Thought
Donald Wiebe

16 Form and Transformation
A Study in the Philosophy of Plotinus
Frederic M. Schroeder

FORM AND TRANSFORMATION
A Study in the Philosophy of Plotinus

Frederic M. Schroeder

McGill-Queen's University Press
Montreal & Kingston • London • Buffalo

© McGill-Queen's University Press 1992
ISBN 0-7735-1016-8
Legal deposit second quarter 1992
Bibliothèque nationale du Québec

Printed in Canada on acid-free paper

This book has been published with the help of a grant from the
Canadian Federation for the Humanities, using funds provided by
the Social Sciences and Humanities Research Council of Canada.
Funding has also been provided by the Faculty of Arts and Science
and the School of Graduate Studies and Research,
Queen's University.

Canadian Cataloguing in Publication Data

Schroeder, Frederic M., 1937–
Form and transformation

(McGill-Queen's studies in the history of ideas; 16)
Includes bibliographical references and index.
ISBN 0-7735-1016-8

1. Plotinus–Contributions in metaphysics.
2. Form (Philosophy). I. Title. II. Series

B693.Z7S37 1992   186'.4   C92-090094-1

This book was typeset by Typo Litho composition inc.
in 10/12 Baskerville.

For Carol

Contents

Preface xi

Acknowledgments xiii

I Form 3

II Light 24

III Silence 40

IV Word 66

V Love 91

Bibliography 115

Index locorum 121

General index 123

Preface

THE PRESENT WORK IS offered as a reflective study of the philosophy of Plotinus. Plotinus nowhere clearly sets forth a metaphysical system. This is not a failure on his part, but rather a mark of his salutary openness to fresh enquiry and experience. It is therefore no purpose of this monograph to "reconstruct" such a system. It is hoped instead that the thread of discussion, departing from a basic insight into Plotinus' understanding of the Platonic Form, will lead the reader exponentially into Plotinus' manner of philosophizing.

This study prescinds from questions of source research, historical location, and the examination of philological cruces for their own sake in presenting its interpretation of the Plotinian text. Words and concepts have been analysed to show how they function synergistically in the semantic fields of Plotinus' enquiry. I hope that the philosopher, the theologian, the student of religion, and the general classicist will find my approach a good introduction to this author and that scholars may find Plotinus to be of intrinsic interest, quite apart from the question of his undoubted influence on the subsequent course of philosophy and theology.

Two recent bibliographies, one by Henry Blumenthal, the other by Kevin Corrigan and Padraig O'Cleirigh (both listed in my bibliography), should exonerate me from providing bibliography for works other than those that I mention in my text and notes. Citations in the notes will be by author and date. Unless otherwise indicated, the translations are from A. H. Armstrong.

The references to the text of Plotinus are of the style now standard among Plotinian scholars. However, a note of explanation might be helpful for those who are not familiar with it. Plotinus' disciple Porphyry edited his works into six collections entitled Enneads (from the Greek word *enneas*, meaning "body of nine"). Each Ennead contains nine tractates, further divided into chapters. Porphyry also informs us of the chronological order of the tractates, which is different from the order in which he published them. A sample reference would be: 1.6 [1].1.1–10. The first number refers to the first Ennead, the second to the sixth tractate in that Ennead, the third (in square brackets) to the number of the tractate in the chronological order, the fourth to the chapter within the tractate, and the last two numbers to the relevant line numbers in the chapter.

The Armstrong translation of Plotinus (A. H. Armstrong, *Plotinus*. 7 vols. Heinemann: London and Cambridge, Mass., 1966–88) will be referred to in the notes as "Armstrong." The Harder-Beutler-Theiler translation and commentary on Plotinus (R. Harder, continued by R. Beutler and W. Theiler, *Plotins Schriften*. 5 vols. Hamburg: Felix Meiner 1956–60) will be referred to in the notes as "HBT." The MacKenna translation of Plotinus (Stephen MacKenna, *Plotinus, The Enneads*, third edition revised by B. S. Page. London: Faber and Faber, 1962) will be referred to in the notes as "MacKenna." The Sleeman and Pollet lexicon to Plotinus (J. H. Sleeman, and G. Pollet, *Lexicon Plotinianum*. Leiden and Louvain: E. J. Brill, Leiden and Leuven University Press, 1980) will be referred to in the notes as "Sleeman and Pollet." H. F. A. von Arnim (ed.), *Stoicorum Veterum Fragmenta*. 4 vols. Leipzig: Teubner, 1903–1924, will be referred to in the notes as "SVF." The Henry and Schwyzer *editio minor* of Plotinus (P. Henry and H.-R. Schwyzer, *Plotini Opera*. 3 vols. Oxford: Oxford University Press, 1964–82), the text of which is the subject of all Plotinus references, will be cited as "H-S."

Acknowledgments

I WISH TO THANK Queen's University at Kingston for granting me sabbatical leave during 1988/89 and the Advisory Research Committee of Queen's University for their support in this project, substantially completed during my sabbatical leave in that year. I wish also to express my gratitude to the Social Sciences and Humanities Research Council of Canada, the German Academic Exchange Service, and the Advisory Research Committee of Queen's University for their support of those of my previous publications that have served as background to the present work and to the Aid to Publications Programme of the Canadian Federation for the Humanities, and to Queen's University for their financial support for the publication of this book.

I wish to express my profound gratitude to Kevin Corrigan and Graeme Nicholson, who both read the book in manuscript, for their helpful criticisms and encouragement. I gratefully acknowledge the comments of the readers both for the McGill-Queen's Press and for the Grant in Aid of Publications Programme of the Canadian Federation for the Humanities. I would also like to thank my colleague Ross Kilpatrick very much for his unfailing support of this project. Special thanks are also due to my colleague Margaret Reesor for her constant friendship throughout my scholarly career. Of course, any remaining faults are entirely my own responsibility.

I wish to express sincere thanks to Werner Beierwaltes, that excellent student of Neoplatonism, who was twice my kind host in Germany, in 1980 and 1982, and to the Albert-Ludwigs-Universität Freiburg-im-Breisgau, where I was his guest. Also to John Fitzgerald, Director of Honors and Privileged Studies at the University of Miami, for his gracious hospitality during my sabbatical year 1988/89, to

Ramón Lemos of that university for permitting me to participate in his fine seminar on phenomenology, and to the University of Miami who entertained me as Visiting Scholar during that year.

I also wish to express my deep thanks to my dear wife Carol Roberts for her unfailing love, support, and patience.

FORM AND TRANSFORMATION

I

Form

WE ARE USED TO THE ANALOGY or metaphor of light in metaphysical and religious discourse. We are perhaps ready to accept that the Platonic Good should be the sun of the intelligible universe or that Christ should be the light of the world. In Plotinus, however, we find a thinker who asks us to understand sensible light and the phenomenon of earthly illumination in terms of the seemingly less palpable procession of soul from soul, as if the events of the spirit were somehow more familiar than our quotidian experience.

Light is, for Plotinus, an effect of the luminous source. Its existence has no dependence upon the object to be illumined, although it is manifested in such an object. Similarly, reflection, itself an instance of illumination, requires no mirror, no reflective surface for its existence, but only for its appearance.[1] In explaining this theory of illumination, Plotinus offers what is meant to be an instructive analogy: "So it is in the case of soul, considered as the activity of a prior soul, that as long as the prior soul abides, so does the subsequent activity" (4.5[29].7.49–51). Plotinus, in a discussion of the light which we behold with our eyes, offers as illustration the procession of lower from higher soul, with the higher soul acting as unique source of that procession. This is meant to clarify how light is an effect its source alone.

Of fire, Plotinus says that it "shines and glitters as if it was a Form" (1.6 [1].3.25–26). Here the luminosity of sensible fire is illustrated by reference to Form. Again, we might be prepared for a Platonic use of fire to describe the luminous character of Form. Yet Plotinus here

---

1. Plotinus 4.5 [29].7.33–49.

also shows that for him the world of Form, the realm of the spirit, is the primary object of experience with reference to which we may understand the sensible world. Rather than using the world of our ordinary waking consciousness as a fund of anagogical metaphor or analogy that may point to and illumine the uncharted territories of the spirit, Plotinus seems cast, shipwrecked and blinking, into the world addressed by sense, a world that can be comprehended only through an orientation toward that other country from which his soul has so precipitously and unpardonably descended.

The contemporary student of Plato will tell us that (if we entertain the Platonic theory of Forms at all) the Platonic Form is posited as cause or explanation. Ontologically it is the cause of being, epistemologically it is the cause of knowledge, and ethically it is the guarantee of right action. The same scholar will find somewhat embarrassing the Platonic description of Form as an object of ecstatic experience, cast in the language of erotic passion and intoxication. By contrast, for Plotinus as a student of Plato the Platonic Form is, first and foremost, an intrinsically valuable object of intellective and spiritual vision. Form is indeed cause. Yet to understand how it is cause, it is crucial first to comprehend it as an intrinsically valuable object of vision, apart from its uses in explanation. The disjunction that we would introduce between rational enquiry and ecstasy is not valid for an understanding of the Plotinian Plato.

The existence of Form is not postulated merely as a means of explanation. Rather Form is in some sense actually experienced by the soul of man. For the purposes of the present discussion, we may interpret the word "experience" broadly, reserving consideration of the nature of this experience for later. That Form is an object of experience may explain why, in the examples we have discussed, Plotinus is prepared to illustrate the phenomena of physics by means of metaphysical examples.

Where Plato will describe the ecstatic experience of Form in the third person, Plotinus is prepared to use the first person:[2]

Many times it has happened: lifted out of the body into myself; becoming external to all other things and self-encentered; beholding a marvellous beauty; then, more than ever, assured of community with the loftiest order;

2. Trans. MacKenna.

enacting the noblest life, acquiring identity with the divine; stationing within It by having attained that activity; poised above whatsoever within the Intellectual is less than the Supreme: yet there comes the moment of descent from intellection to reasoning, and after that sojourn in the divine, I ask myself how it happens that I can now be descending, and how did the Soul ever enter into my body, the Soul which, even within the body, is the high thing it has shown itself to be (4.8 [6].1.1–11).

In Plato's *Symposium*[3] the wise woman of Mantineia says of the vision of Beauty, "something marvellous is beheld, by nature beautiful" (κατόψεται τι θαυμαστὸν τὴν φύσιν καλόν). Plotinus echoes her words[4] in his claim, "beholding a beauty wonderfully great" (θαυμαστὸν ἡλίκον ὁρῶν κάλλος). This is also the only place in which Plotinus makes use of the first person to describe the human experience of Form. Yet the use of the first person in this passage surely allows us to see that he does not merely entertain the possibility of such experience: for him it is a reality. His appeal to tradition, in the reference to Plato's *Symposium*, intends a catholic validation of his experience.[5] Furthermore, this passage invites us to interpret other passages where Plotinus discusses such awareness in the third person as a serious address to the reach of human experience.[6]

Armstrong's translation, with its use of the indicative mood ("Often I have woken up out of the body and have entered into myself..."), yields the sense that the experience is an interruption of everyday life. As O'Meara suggests, the MacKenna translation (which I have used here) preserves Plotinus' participles (ἐγειρόμενος...γενόμενος) and gives the sense that Plotinus is describing the continuous and timeless experience of the higher soul which is interrupted by the commerce of the soul with the body. This reading of the text would

3. 210e4–5
4. 4.8 [6].1.3.
5. Cf. Armstrong, "Tradition, Reason and Experience," for a fine discussion of this matter.
6. Porphyry, the disciple and biographer of Plotinus, affirms that his master achieved union with the One four times while in his presence. We may not place great faith in Porphyry's account, *Vita Plotini* 23.15–18: see Schroeder, "Ammonius Saccas," on the credibility of Porphyry's biography. Porphyry, a late-comer to the Plotinian circle, is attempting to establish his place as the successor of Plotinus. The language of Porphyry's description reflects 4.8 [6].1.

support the view that Plotinus' primary orientation is toward the intelligible world.[7]

In Plato's *Phaedo* Simmias is exhorted not to employ sight, or any other sense, but only intellect in the address to Form.[8] In the analogy of the sun and the Good in the *Republic* the Good is said to have the same relationship to the objects of knowledge which the sun bears toward things visible.[9] The Good rules over the realm of what is known, even as the sun is lord of the visible.[10] In the passage concerning the Divided Line, the fundamental division is between what is visible and what is intelligible.[11] We may think the Forms, but cannot see them.[12]

On the other hand, in the *Symposium*[13] and in the *Phaedrus*,[14] the Forms are addressed by vision. We may ask whether these statements do not contradict Plato's insistence elsewhere that the Forms are to be known only by intellection to the exclusion of vision. Or is Plato here using the language of sight metaphorically?

Note that this language of vision in the *Symposium* and *Phaedrus* is accompanied by expressions of ecstasy. Thus the famous pages 210 and 211 of the *Symposium* describe Beauty as the crowning object of eros. In the *Phaedrus* the vision of the Plain of Truth belongs both to eros and madness.[15]

It would be easy to multiply instances in which Plotinus joins ecstatic imagery, borrowed from Plato, of erotic passion, intoxication, and madness with the vision of Form as intrinsically valuable object of vision. Plotinus contrasts Intellect's power of self-contemplation with its capacity of beholding the One: "And that first one is the contemplation of Intellect in its right mind, and the other is Intellect in love, when it goes out of its mind 'drunk with nectar'; then it falls in love, simplified into happiness by having its fill" (6.7 [38].35.24–26). The drunkenness here is that of Plenty in the myth of Poverty and Plenty

7. Cf. O'Meara, "A propos un témoignage," for this interpretation. O'Meara compares 6.9 [9].9.55 – 10.3.

8. 65e6–66a8.

9. 509b2–10.

10. *Republic* 509d1–3.

11. *Republic* 509d8.

12. *Republic* 507b9–10.

13. 210d3–4; 210e4; 211b6; 211d2–3.

14. 247c7–8, d3, 5–6; 248c3; 249e5; 250c4.

15. 249d4–250c6.

in the *Symposium*.[16] Also present, of course, are the themes of erotic passion and madness familiar from the *Symposium* and *Phaedrus*.

In the *Phaedrus* the place above the heavens may be beheld only by reason, charioteer of the soul.[17] This statement would suggest that the language of vision here is used metaphorically. Elsewhere in the *Phaedrus*, however, it is stated that Beauty is unique among the Forms in that it can be beheld by sight.[18] For Plotinus Beauty is greatly evident to the sense of vision but also manifests itself to those who mount upward from the world of sense.[19]

Plotinus seems to seize upon the Platonic language of ecstatic vision to reverse the proportions of the Divided Line. He declares the anagogical power of love:

> But if someone who sees beauty excellently represented in a face is carried to that higher world, will anyone be so sluggish in mind and so immovable that, when he sees all the beauties in the world of sense, all its good proportion and the mighty excellence of its order, and the splendour of form which is manifested in the stars, for all their remoteness, he will not thereupon think, seized with reverence, "What wonders, and from what a source?" If he did not, he would neither have understood (κατενόησεν) this world here nor seen (εἶδεν) that higher world. (2.9 [33].16.48–56)

Notice the inversion of sense and intellection in the last sentence. Here, as in Plato, the vision of Form is joined with erotic ecstasy.[20]

In the next chapter, we shall be examining the dynamic continuity that exists between the sensible and intelligible worlds. We may here examine a text which asserts this continuity:

> The greatest beauty in the world of sense, therefore, is a manifestation of the noblest among the intelligibles, of their power and of their goodness, and

---

16. 203b5.
17. 247c7–8.
18. 250d3–e1.
19. 1.6 [1].1.
20. Cf. Schwyzer, "Plotinus," cols. 526–27 and 1.4 [46].10.14; 6.9 [9].5.12 on how Intellect may be beheld as if it were an object of sensation; Bréhier, *La Philosophie de Plotin*, xi–xii, observes: "C'est trop peu de dire que Plotin a le sentiment du monde intelligible: C'est plutôt chez lui sensualité;" cf. 6.7 [38].6.1–9; *ibid.* 12.23–30 and Hadot, "Structure et Thèmes," 647–48.

all things are held together forever, those which exist intelligibly and those which exist perceptibly (συνέχεται πάντα εἰσαεὶ τά τε νοητῶς τά τε αἰσθητῶς ὄντα), the intelligibles existing of themselves and the things perceived by the senses receiving their existence for ever by participation in them, imitating the intelligible nature as far as they can. (4.8 [6].6.23–28)

This continuity between the worlds is further suggested by the statement: "Sensations here are dim intellections; intellections there are vivid sensations" (6.7 [38].7.30–31). If there is no radical disjunction between sensation and intellection, then surely the use of words implying vision is not really out of place in describing the experience of Form. Indeed, if sensation and intellection are at two ends of a continuum, the one an intensification of the other, the use of the language of vision may belong to something more than metaphor.

In the middle dialogues, Plato uses the language of participation to explain how the Form functions as cause.[21] Plato himself subjects this incautious language to aporetic scrutiny in the "day and sail" argument of the *Parmenides*.[22] If the Form is wholly present in the many particulars, which are separate from it, Parmenides argues that it will be separated from itself and lose its identity. Socrates answers that day may be wholly present to different places and yet not lose its identity in this manner. Parmenides rejoins that if the Form of Largeness (μέγεθος) is present to the large particulars as a sail is stretched out over the heads of sailors, then a part (μέρος) and not the whole Form will be present to each particular. The Form will be divided (μερίζεσθαι) among the many particulars and will thus lose its unity. It will also sacrifice its integrity and hence identity. The Large will become small.

The youthful Socrates may be seen as naive in allowing the older and more experienced Parmenides to substitute the "sail" analogy for the imagery of "day" that Socrates had advanced earlier.[23] If the Form is present to the many particulars as day is present to Athens and Sparta, it need not be divided. Indeed, whether we view "day" as a unit of time or as daylight it will be immaterial and hence indivisible.

21. *Phaedo* 101c; 102b; *Symposium* 211b; *Republic* 476d.
22. 130e5–131e7.
23. *Parmenides* 131b3–6.

Thus Plotinus (who construes "day" as "daylight") interprets the "day and sail" argument.[24]

While Plotinus believes that the force of the "day and sail" argument of the Platonic *Parmenides* may be overcome, he does not think that the acceptance of that argument rests on a simple human error. Rather, when we accept Parmenides' reasoning and divide the Form we participate in a grander scheme of misapprehension. The hypostasis of Intellect cannot maintain its vision of the One in primal unity, but "being unable to preserve the power which it was procuring, it broke it up and made the one [power] into many that it might bear it part by part (κατὰ μέρος)" (6.7 [38].15.20–22). In so doing, Intellect constitutes itself as an imitation of the Good, as a many-hued and variegated Good (ἀγαθὸν ποικίλον, 6.7 [38].15.24). Here the language of division reflects the "day and sail" argument. Yet Intellect does not succeed in dividing the One. Rather, in its very failure to divide the indivisible One, it constitutes itself as the One in division. We may compare 5.1 [10].7.17–18: "But Intellect sees, by means of itself, like something divided proceeding from the undivided (μεριστῷ ἐξ ἀμερίστου)." In this passage as well, Intellect constitutes itself in the attempt to divide the unity and identity of the One.[25]

---

24. Cf. Plotinus 6.4 [22].7–8, 3.8 [30].10, and Schroeder, "The Platonic *Parmenides*," 51–54. It appears that Plotinus interprets "day" here as "daylight", cf. Plotinus 6.9 [9].4.10–11 and Schroeder "The Platonic *Parmenides*," 53 note 4. The soul and the intelligible world with which it is in union together constitute true light, which is not measured by largeness (μέγεθος) and is greater than all quantity, 1.6 [1].9.15–22. This latter passage is especially interesting. Platonic scholars who can accept the notion of a Form of Beauty will find it difficult to cope with the notion of the Form of something apparently relative, such as Largeness. Here the Largeness (perhaps we should render it "greatness") of the intelligible world, being itself the foundation of any judgment of size, extent, or degree in the sensible world, is not subject to the relativistic measurement which belongs to the latter realm. Light is a suitable construal here as it is incorporeal: see Chapter 2, pp. 24, 26–28, 32, 35, 37 below (thus we need not with Fielder, "Plotinus' Reply," insist that it be a unit of time).

25. Cf. Schroeder, "Conversion and Consciousness," on the interpretation of this important chapter. Plotinus appears to read the "day and sail" argument in terms of the *Timaeus* 35a where, in the account of creation, the distinction is drawn between an indivisible intelligible reality and a divisible corporeal reality. A reading of the introductory arguments of the *Parmenides* in terms of the *Timaeus* allows Plotinus to situate their aporetic character in the more positive context of creation, cf. Schroeder, "The Platonic *Parmenides*," 72 note 46.

Similarly, the Soul constitutes itself by dividing the unity and identity of Intellect (which, while it in its relation to the One is many, is, in
its relation to the Soul, one and identical). As participants in Soul, we
share in this division, constituting ourselves as we divide the unity and
identity of Intellect. Plotinus asks, "What then are the things in the
one Intellect which we divide (μερίζομεν) in our thinking?" (5.9
[5].9.1–2). Reflecting that the universe is derived finally from Intellect,
he says: "That which is formed into the universe has its form divided
(εἶδος μεμερισμένον), man in one place and the sun in another; but
the forming nature has all things in one" (14–16). Individual souls
participate then in this division: "The Soul of the All looks toward
Intellect as a whole, but the individual souls rather to their own partial
intellects (τοὺς ἐν μέρει)" (4.3 [27].6.15–17).

Let us reflect upon the significance of this way of interpreting Plato.
Contemporary scholarship may, unlike Plotinus, take the following
view. The doctrine that Form is cause is the heart of the Platonic
enterprise. We may regard the introductory arguments of the *Parmenides* as refuting the Platonic theory of Forms and thus paving the
way for its rejection by Aristotle. We may then dismiss the ecstatic
vision of Form in the *Symposium* and *Phaedrus* as empty poetic ornament. If we further dismiss the God of Aristotle as needless Platonic
baggage, we may see ourselves as set firmly upon the way to establishing philosophy as the handmaiden to science and technology. For
Plotinus, however, the vision of Form is precious. When we divide
the Form, we constitute ourselves and the world around so as to
exclude that vision and that ecstasy. From this viewpoint then the
argument of Plato's *Parmenides* is not descriptive, but performative.
In engaging in the mental processes that would divide the unity of
Form, we constitute ourselves and the world around us as that divided
unity. The "day and sail" argument describes the Form as material
and hence divisible. The cosmic moment of addressing the Form as
if it were material and hence divisible does not merely attempt to
describe its nature, but performs to create another nature, the division
of the sensible and material world.

In the copy-likeness argument of Plato's *Parmenides*, Socrates advances the argument that the particular is a copy (ὁμοίωμα), the Form
the pattern (παράδειγμα) it imitates.[26] Parmenides plays upon the

26. 132c12–133a7.

ambiguity of the Greek word ὅμοιος. As with our English word "like," this word may describe either the symmetrical relation of similarity or the asymmetrical relation of imitation. Parmenides takes it to refer unambiguously to the symmetrical relation of similarity. Thus he asks: if the particular is like the Form, is not the Form also like the particular? Now the Form as pattern was posited in the first instance to explain the similarity among particulars. If the same relationship exists between the particular and the Form, then surely we must posit yet a further Form to account for the similarity between the Form and the particular. Of course, this process may be extended to infinite regress.

For Plotinus, the crucial point of difference between similarity and imitation is epistemological. In the *Phaedo*, Plato analyses the relation between similarity and association, as he argues that all of our learning is really recollection.[27] The beloved comes to mind when the lover sees his lyre or cloak. If we see Simmias, we recall Cebes. Here recollection depends upon a mental act of association which is independent of any intrinsic similarity between the associated items. By contrast, when we see a picture of Simmias, we may recall Simmias himself. In this example, we have not only association, as in the case of the lyre or cloak and the beloved, but also similarity. According to Plato, the recollection of Form requires both association and similarity. We associate the imperfect equality of sticks and stones with the perfect equality of the Form of Equality to which they are similar.

In the *Phaedo* knowledge of Form is ante-natal and experience of particulars only begins at birth.[28] Yet Cebes could see Simmias and the cloak or lyre at the same time and make the same association he would in Simmias' absence. We could also see Simmias and his portrait together and form the same association as when they were apart. Thus, association in general does not require temporal separation and in the specific case of *anamnêsis* such separation may be regarded as incidental.

As the association need not now depend upon separation in time, Plotinus demythologizes the ante-natal character of Form in the *Phaedo*. The association need not be between something that we see now and something that we have seen before birth. Recollection de-

27. 72e-73e.
28. 75a-b.

scribes access to a plane of consciousness which is perpetually addressed to the Forms, but does not always impinge upon our normal waking consciousness.[29] Thus two people may look at the same painting and one will interpret it after the intelligible model and know true love, while the other will see it merely as a likeness of a sensible model.[30]

Imitation, of course, involves the relation of similarity. Yet it differs from other cases of similarity in also requiring association and interpretation. This association demands a pattern of cognitive priority and posteriority. It is because we know the pattern first that we may later know the image (as we have seen, the priority need not be temporal). To maintain the cognitive priority of pattern to copy is to avoid the infinite regress of the copy-likeness argument which reduces pattern and copy to the same explanatory level.

Plotinus distinguishes two senses of "likeness" (ὁμοίωσις), symmetrical and asymmetrical,[31] arising from the relationship between archetype (ἀρχέτυπον) and imitation (μίμημα).[32] Two imitations of the same Form exhibit symmetrical likeness, and the Form and particular, asymmetrical likeness. Thus he can say: "It is they [*sc.* the gods], not men, who are the objects of our imitation (ὁμοίωσις); likeness among men is the resemblance of one image to another when both images are drawn from the same source, but the other kind of likeness is imitation directed toward yet another object beyond them both as to a pattern" (παράδειγμα) (1.2 [19].7.27–30).[33] This passage is an exegesis of the imitation of God in Plato *Theaetetus* 176b.

Let us examine the senses of likeness more closely. We may distinguish between "attributes of similarity" and "attributes of imitation." The subject of a painting has, let us say, blonde curly hair, blue eyes, and an aquiline nose. The painting has a certain shade of yellow paint that corresponds to the colour of the hair, another shade of blue that corresponds to the colour of the eyes, wavy lines to represent the

---

29. Cf. 4.3 [27].25; 4.4 [28].5.1–11; 5.9 [5].5.29–34 and Schroeder, "The Platonic *Parmenides*," 55–56. Plotinus does (3.7 [45].1.23; 4.7 [2].12.9) use *anamnêsis* in the traditional sense as well, but as O'Daly, "Memory in Plotinus," 467 note 3 observes, "that does not lessen the perceptive critique of IV.3.25."

30. 2.9 [33].16.43–48 and Schroeder, "The Platonic *Parmenides*," 56.

31. οὐκ ἀντιστρέφον, 1.2 [19].2.7.

32. 1.2 [19].2.3.

33. My translation.

shape of the hair, straight lines to depict the angle of the nose. In the original there are shades of yellow and blue, wavy and straight lines. These attributes are to be found independently both in the original and in the image and hence may be termed "attributes of similarity." Yet if I look at the painting, I do not merely see such lines and colours. I understand them in terms of their rôle as imitating their subject's attributes, as "curly," "blonde", etc. In their aggregate such characteristics – "attributes of imitation" – make us recollect the model.

Now in the original the attributes of imitation inhere in a unity, the subject herself. To make the image, the artist analyses and divides, as an aquiline nose is resolved into straight lines, blonde hair into a shade of yellow, etc. The image has, in comparison with the model, only a quasi-unity. Plotinus sees here a vital connexion between the division in the "day and sail" argument, which we discussed above, and the reduction of attributes of imitation to attributes of similarity in the copy-likeness argument of the *Parmenides*.

In the "day and sail" argument, the failure to see Form as immaterial results in its division, in the corruption of its unity. In the "copy-likeness" argument, the confusion between likeness as merely the symmetrical relation of similarity and the more pertinent asymmetrical relation of imitation introduces infinite regress. The "day and sail" argument and the "copy-likeness" argument may appear to be separate and distinct, the first addressing the question of unity and the second the question of likeness. Yet Plotinus sees the question of unity in the "copy-likeness" argument as well as in the "day and sail" argument.

If we behold the Form or model in itself, without reference to anything outside itself, or in its intrinsic character, then it is experienced as a unity in which each part is joined to the whole by the interiority of its own relations. When (as in strictly representational art) we analyse the Form or model so that we see it rather as a disparate collection of discrete parts, we sunder its unity. As the individual characteristics are separated out from the unity of the original, the original is, in a sense, divided. Of course, the original is not itself divided. Yet it becomes divided in the sense that its image is a divided version of itself analysed as a multiplicity of attributes the unity of which may only properly be understood with reference to the model.

The "day and sail" argument seems to be ontological in character, the "copy-likeness" argument to be epistemological. Yet in seeing the latter argument to be an explication of the former, Plotinus marries ontology and epistemology. For example, when Soul divides the unity of Intellect into discrete attributes that belie the unity of the original, it constitutes itself and the world as such a spurious and divided unity. It substitutes, as it were, the sail for the day, the material for the immaterial, the discrete and multiple attributes of its analysis for the primal unity that they represent.

Thus the image is a reduction to multiplicity of the unity of the original: "Everything in the intelligible world is substance. Why then is everything in the sensible world not substance too? In the intelligible all is substance because all things are one, but here, because the images are separated, one thing is one thing and another is another" (2.6 [17].1.7–10). Plotinus argues further:

Reality there, when it possesses an individual characteristic of substance, is not qualitative, but when the process of rational thinking separates the distinctive individuality in these realities, not taking it away from the intelligible world but rather grasping it and producing something else, it produces the qualitative as a kind of part of substance, grasping what appears on the surface of the reality. (2.6 [17].3.10–20)

The mind analyses intelligible substance into discrete qualities and thus divides it and creates the sensible world as its quasi-unitary image.

In 6.3 [44].15 Plotinus argues that the sensible world as a whole bears an adjectival relationship to the intelligible world which stands as substance to the sensible world as quality. Thus Man in the intelligible world is described by man in the sensible world. This is illustrated by the relation of Socrates and his portrait. The portrait shares attributes of similarity with Socrates. Although everything in the portrait describes Socrates, it is not him. The One is said (5.3 [49].15.31–32) to have the attributes of Intellect, but in such a way that they are not discrete; these are, however, discrete in Intellect.[34]

The hypostasis of Intellect, as we have seen, constitutes itself in the act of attempting to divide the One. We may now understand that this division is ineluctably connected with an act of representation and reduction. Intellect resolves attributes which inhere in unity in the One into a plurality of characteristics that in their aggregate present an image of the One. In the act of analysing the One into attributes

---

34. Cf. Schroeder, "The Platonic *Parmenides*," 67–68.

of similarity, Intellect does not divide the One itself. Rather Intellect constitutes itself as an image in manyness of the One, an image made up of many parts.[35] The One, of course, remains undivided and its character as pattern remains intact and it is not confused with its image. Thus the "day and sail" and the "copy-likeness" arguments are met. These arguments are curiously successful. Intellect, in dividing the One and reducing it to the status of its image, which is Intellect itself, executes the steps of these arguments performatively in an act of self-constitution. In so far as we are co-participants with Intellect and then Soul in the creation of the universe, we also participate in the cosmic rehearsal of these arguments. Our acceptance of these arguments as philosophers reflects the fall of the Soul and with it of our own souls.

An analogous relationship holds between Intellect and the Soul.[36] Soul creates a series of images as it descends "deceived by likeness"[37] to the world of sense. We may recall that the copy-likeness argument of the *Parmenides* leads to infinite regress, an endless multiplication of Forms. The Soul, in its restless analysis and division of Form, produces ever new Forms, but Forms which are inferior, not superior to the analysandum. Man in the sensible world is the last product of Soul's sequential analysis of the Form of Man: "Man in the intelligible world is man before all men. He shines forth upon the second man and the second man shines forth upon the third" (6.7 [38].6.11–13).[38]

Both the "day and sail" argument, with its account of participation, and the "copy-likeness" argument, with its concern with likeness, proceed from a myopic interest in the Form only as cause and hence are unsuccessful. For Plotinus the Platonic understanding of the Form as intrinsically valuable object of ecstatic vision is not a poetic ornament to be set aside from Form as cause or explanation. We may, in Plotinus' reception of the Platonic theory of Forms, distinguish between the

35. In 5.3 [49].13.30–31, Intellect is said to have manyness as an image in relation to an archetype.

36. Soul, an image of Intellect, looks toward Intellect and thus becomes an image of Intellect, just as Intellect looks toward the One that it may be Intellect, 5.1 [10].6.46–48.

37. 4.6 [41].3.9.

38. My translation. Perhaps this is a trace of the "Third Man" argument of Plato's *Parmenides* 131e8–132b1 which Fielder, "A Plotinian View," 339, claims is not found in Plotinus; cf. Schroeder, "The Platonic *Parmenides*," 71.

two moments of use and enjoyment. When we speak of the Form as cause or explanation, we are thinking of it in terms of use. When we address it as an intrinsically valuable object of intellective or spiritual vision, we are considering it in respect of enjoyment. In this scheme, enjoyment has priority over use. Indeed use may be seen as the corruption of enjoyment.[39] So to argue about Form only in terms of use is to engage in a self-defeating project, as the above has shown.

We have seen that Plotinus, by contrast, does not allow the Form to become sundered in its relationship to particulars. He is equally careful that it should not lose its unity and identity through its relations with other Forms. Thus Justice is beautiful, and Beauty is just, but not in such a way that a part of justice is assigned to beauty or *vice versa*. Each Form contains all the other Forms in the interiority of its own relations, i.e., all relations in Intellect are internal.[40] Thus "Each there has everything in itself and sees all things in every other, so that all are everywhere and each and every one is all and the glory is unbounded; for each of them is great, because even the small is great; the sun there is all the stars, and each star is the sun and all the others" (5.8 [31].4.6–10). We can see that here too the Form of Largeness does not become divided, as in the "day and sail" argument of the Plato's *Parmenides*. Thus even the small is great and does not divide the greatness of the intelligible world.

We use the Form as a means of explaining the character of the particulars that either participate in it or imitate it. Yet after we have used the Form as an instrument of explanation, we are left with other questions when we consider the Form, not just as a pattern or model posited for the sake of explanation, but in its intrinsic character. In his interpretation of Plato's *Timaeus*, Plotinus pursues such a line of enquiry. Plotinus, in an interpretation of Plato's *Timaeus* 45d-e, where the mortal body is equipped with vision, argues that men and other creatures are provided with the senses that they might be saved from

---

39. On the Plotinian response to the aporetic arguments addressed to the Platonic Theory of Forms in the Platonic *Parmenides,* cf. further Fielder, "Plotinus' Copy Theory," "Plotinus' Reply," "A Plotinian view." Where my position is epistemological, or rather, hermeneutical, Fielder is narrowly ontological, but see Fielder, "Plotinus' Copy Theory," 6: "In his treatment of the likeness of eikon to Form Plotinus is strongly influenced by his personal experience of the intelligible world."

40. Cf. 5.5 [32].1.28–43; 5.8 [31].3.30–4.11; 5.9 [5].8.3–7 and Trouillard, "The Logic of Attribution," for an excellent discussion of this doctrine.

destruction (σῴζοιτο) (6.7 [38].1.1–5).⁴¹ However, if the senses are required here for safety, do they then belong to Form which would scarcely require such immunity? In the sensible world, things are separated out in such a way that we dissociate fact and cause. Aristotle argues that we must know the fact of a thing's existence (τὸ ὅτι) before we may know its reason (τὸ διότι).⁴² However, despite this cognitive priority, argues Aristotle, it can happen that we in fact know both that something exists and why it exists in the same moment of enquiry. For example, an eclipse is the obstruction of the moon by the earth. Here definition of what an eclipse is and an explanation of why it is coincide.⁴³

For Plotinus there is no planning of the order of the sensible world on the part of the Demiurge or his children,⁴⁴ as if the intelligible world were a blueprint for creation drafted by the operations of discursive thought. Thus: "How could the alone, the one, the simple contain in explication the 'this, so that we may not have that' and 'it was intending this, if that could not be' and 'the useful appeared and became salvific (σωτήριον)'" (6.7 [38].1.39–42).⁴⁵ In the intelligible world, "that" and "why" coalesce. In the sensible world, when we ask the question "Why does man have sight?", we separate "man" and "sight." In the intelligible world, fact (τὸ ὅτι) and reason (τὸ διὰ τί) necessarily coincide. Thus by reference to the latter we see, in the case both of man and his sight, that these exist not for some external reason (such as safety) but for completeness (6.7 [38].2.1–11).

Plotinus offers Aristotle's example of an eclipse to show that the coalescence of fact and reason may be observed in the sensible world.⁴⁶ Plotinus asks further: "Why should there be eyes there? That there might be all. And why eyebrows? That there might be all. For indeed if you would say 'for the sake of safety (σωτηρία),' you would mean that it is an indwelling protection of essence; this [cause] would be

41. For further aspects of the dependence of this passage on the *Timaeus* see HBT 3 b 481–2.

42. *Posterior Analytics* ii.8.93a17–21.

43. *Posterior Analytics* ii.8.93a29–68.

44. Plotinus refers to "God or some god" (6.7 [38].1.1) because, in Plato *Timaeus* 42e5 ff. the Demiurge leaves the creation of the mortal bodies to his children.

45. My translation.

46. 6.7 [38].2.11–12; on Plotinus' use of these passages from Aristotle *Posterior Analytics* here see Matter, *Einfluss des "Timaeus,"* 115–16.

something contributing [to essence]. Thus essence is prior to cause
and cause is a part of essence" (6.7 [38].3.14–18).[47] Thus the cause
or reason inherent in Form is the reason for its being simply what it
is. Indeed, the possibility that fact and reason could be disjoined
results from the divisive descent from the world of Form. Plotinus
invests σωτηρία not only with the meaning of "safety" but with the
more positive sense of "salvation."

Plotinus asks: "What would horns be there [i.e., in the intelligible
world] for defense? Indeed they serve toward the self-sufficiency as
of an animal and perfection" (6.7 [38].10.1–2).[48] If we were to ask a
child drawing a picture of an ox, "Why does the ox have horns?", the
child would doubtless reply, "Because it is an ox," not "For defense."
Plotinus would be on the side of the child.[49]

The absorption of cause into essence, of "why" into "that," again
demonstrates that Form is of intrinsic value and as such is the object,
rather than the instrument, of our quest. Let us return for the moment
to the example of the ox. We say that the ox in the sensible world
has horns for defense. In the intelligible world, it has horns for the
sake of completeness. In the second chapter we shall see that Form
and particular are ends of a continuum. We may expect that if I

---

47. My translation. In the *Timaeus* 45d7–8, Plato argues that the eyelid was created
as the safeguard (σωτηρία) of sight. While the reference is to eyelids rather than
eyes and eyebrows, it is difficult to deny that Plotinus has this passage in mind.
HBT 3 b 485 compares Aristotle's *De partibus animalium* ii.658b14–15: αἱ ὀφρύες καὶ αἱ
βλεφαρίδες – βοηθείας χάριν εἰσιν.

48. My translation.

49. Cf. Hadot, "Structure et Thèmes," especially 646–50. Hadot prefaces (625) his
excellent study of 6.7 [38] with the following quotations from Angelus Silesius:

Die Rose, welche hier dein äussres Auge sieht
Die hat von Ewigkeit in Gott also geblüht.

(*Cherubinischer Wandersmann, Sämtliche Poetische Werke*, vol. 1, poem 108; I quote these
verses here as they are produced in Helm's edition).

Die Ros' ist ohn warum; sie blühet, weil sie blühet,
Sie acht nicht ihrer selbst, fragt nicht ob man sie siehet.

(*ibid.* vol. 1, poem 289).

It is difficult to imagine that Hadot has not Heidegger's *Satz vom Grund* in mind here
(see Heidegger, *Satz vom Grund*, 63–75 on the meaning of these verses).

contemplate an ox in the sensible world in terms of enjoyment, rather than merely of use, I shall not only better appreciate the animal but shall begin my journey toward the vision of Form.

Plotinus is careful to protect Form against the loss of unity and identity. It is not to be divided among the particulars. It is also not to be divided or parcelled out among the other Forms. As we have seen, each Form in Intellect contains all the other Forms in the interiority of its own relations, so that, if Justice is beautiful, it is not the case that a part of Beauty is attached to Justice.

This way of looking at things may also be applied to the world of particulars. The particular may, in its uses or relationships, be plundered of its unity and identity. If the ox has horns only to defend itself against other animals, or vision only to keep it from bumping into things, then the attributes of horns and vision are divided or distributed among these external purposes. If we look at the ox with the eyes of an artist whose goal transcends mere representation, but is some imitation not based on analytical division, we may see that it has these attributes in order to be itself. This is precisely what Plotinus says of the Form.

If we look at the particular in its relation to the Form, restricting the role of the Form to causation, we may also rob the particular of unity and identity. Thus we may say that the ox is ox by its participation in Oxness. For the purpose of this claim, my ox is now one ox among other oxen. The ground of this line of questioning is comparison with other oxen, rather than investigation of the universe of possible discourse about this ox. The same limitation would follow on use of the language of likeness. The ascent to the enjoyment of Form would not arise from this act of discursive comparison. It belongs rather to my openness to the self-manifestation of the particular in its unity, identity, and uniqueness.

Plotinus, in his treatise *On Destiny*, argues that the human soul, free of the body, is cut loose from the cosmic web of destiny and causation (κοσμικῆς αἰτίας ἔξω, 3.1 [3].8.9–11). Even as the ox becomes free to be that very ox for us when we consider it in its intrinsic value, so are we first free when we in so considering it stand outside that order of things which would strip us of our independent worth. We may deduce from this argument that "body" (σῶμα) refers not just to the individual tenement of clay but also to our servile entrapment in the toils of fate and providence which would scatter us among their various uses and purposes consequent upon embodiment. The assertion of the soul's freedom from body would then be a liberation from such heteronomous cosmic deployment of our gifts and resources. That freedom in turn allows us to become co-determinants in the order of the cosmos (lines 17–20). We are invited to think that the freedom of the human soul may be developed by an appropriate way of looking at the particular in its intrinsic value.

Plotinus argues[50] against the Stoic position that beauty arises from proportion.[51] If that were so, he maintains, then simple things, such as lightning in the night sky, or stars, or gold, would not be beautiful. Where is there proportion or composition in these things? Moreover, in composite things, beauty does not arise from proportion alone. Thus in a musical composition each separate sound may in itself be beautiful. "Sometimes," says Plotinus, "art gives beauty to a whole house with its parts, and sometimes nature gives beauty to a single stone."[52]

It is not so much that the Form of Beauty is offered as a generic explanation for the many instances of beauty. Rather Plotinus stresses the actual participation in Beauty by any beautiful object. Any manifestation of beauty, whether it occurs in musical or architectural composition or in the simplicity of a sound or a stone, invites us, on each occasion, to seek its ground in the Form of Beauty.

Beauty is grounded only in Beauty itself. Thus "When, though the same good proportion is there all the time, the same face appears beautiful and sometimes does not, surely we must say that being beautiful is something else over and above good proportion, and good proportion is beautiful because of something else" (1.6 [1].1.37–40).[53] Beauty may at one time manifest itself in something of constant arrangement or proportions, at another time not. This fact demonstrates that we are not merely positing the Form of Beauty to explain the occurrence of things which (on the basis of some criterion other than the Form, *viz.* proportion) have already been agreed to be beautiful. It is rather the case that the mystery of any manifestation of

---

50. 1.6 [1].1.

51. Cf. svf III 278 (=Stobaeus *Ecl.* ii.62.15), especially lines 31–44 in *SVF*; *SVF* III.279 (=Cicero *Tusculan Disputations* iv.13.30–31), especially 4.13.31; cf. St Augustine *De Civitate Dei* xxii.19; cf. HBT Ib 369; Armstrong trans. 1. 6 [1].1, p. 234 note 1.

52. 1.6 [1].2.25–27.

53. Cf. 6.7 [38].22.22–24; 27–28.

Beauty can only be understood by an appeal to the Form of Beauty. We shall later see that this appeal is existential.[54]

If we think of a beautiful face as one that fulfills certain established aesthetic norms such as proportion, we may risk ignoring the contribution of facial expression the beauty of which may not be so analysable. Plotinus may, on the argument we have been examining, provide us with the first theory of facial expression. It is relevant to note that he, unlike Plato, regards the face as a unity. In the *Protagoras* of Plato, it is asked whether virtue is one, like gold, or many, as a face?[55] As we think of a face primarily in terms of expression, i.e., not merely as a jumble of parts, eyes, nose, mouth, etc., this comparison strikes us as strange. Discussing whether the object of perception is one or many, Plotinus asks us to assume that it is one, like a face.[56] Thus, unlike Plato, he appeals to the face as united by a single expression at a time. The example of the face that is sometimes beautiful, at other times not, despite its proportions, also invokes the Plotinian theory of expression. Beauty, as elusive as a smile, evades generic classification. It may yet summon us to the ground of all beauty.

Plotinus' view of perspective affords valuable insight into his defense of the intrinsic value of the particular as an object of contemplation. Plotinus asks[57] why it is that distant objects appear to be smaller? What the eye perceives is colour primarily and size only incidentally.[58] In the case of distant objects, blurring in colour is accompanied by diminution in size. When we see an object up close, we can, in the presence of all of its details and its distinct colours,

54. Anton, "Plotinus' Refutation of Beauty as Symmetry," maintains that Plotinus' arguments against symmetry as the ground of beauty are not altogether convincing. The statement (1.6 [1].1.28–29) that the parts must themselves be beautiful for there to be beauty in the whole may be too dogmatic. Plotinus himself rejects this argument in 3.2 [47].17.64–74. But as Armstrong, "Beauty and the Discovery of Divinity," 157, remarks, "if the implicit contrast is not simply between 'proportion' and 'form' but between proportion and colour considered abstractly as the conformity of a lifeless thing to certain aesthetic rules," then the argument may make good sense. The thrust of the argument is not to offer an "atomic" (Anton) as opposed to a "symmetrical" theory of beauty, but to argue aporetically that there is no aesthetic theory which will offer an exhaustive explanation of beauty.

55. 329d5.

56. Cf. 4.7 [2].6.19–20 and Schaerer *ap.* Henry, "Une comparaison," 445.

57. 2.8 [35].1.

58. Cf. Armstrong translation, introductory note, 209.

judge its true size. When it is far off, we know that it is coloured, but not how large a space is coloured. An example of how to measure size is provided by a landscape of many and varied objects. The extent of the whole may be measured from the individual parts. This way of looking at size and distance implies a rejection of geometrical perspective.

This view of perspective rests upon a fundamental tenet of Plotinian optics. Plotinus denies that the organ of vision receives an impression of the object seen. The image is rather located in the object seen.[59] Sight is not a passive affection proceeding from the object to the eye, that is thereby affected, but an act on our part directed towards the object.[60]

The eye, itself luminous, directs its light to meet with the light and colours (themselves lights) of its object of perception and declares that what is below light is dark and material.[61] We may deduce that, for Plotinus, the eye would abolish darkness and, with it, differences in luminous emphasis which would describe spatial differentiation and create perspective. The object is rendered transparent by a vision that is itself transparent.

We may recall that, in Intellect, each Form contains the other Forms in the interiority of its own relations. Each of these Forms is itself also an intellect. Thus:

They see all things, not those to which coming to be, but those to which real being belongs, and they see themselves in other things; for all things there are transparent, and there is nothing dark or opaque; everything and all things are clear to the inmost part to everything; for light is transparent to light. Each there has everything in itself and sees all things in every other, so that all are everywhere and each and every one is all and the glory is unbounded. (5.8 [31].4.3–8)

This passage offers a model from the intelligible world of how (in attenuation and distance) vision takes place in the world of sense. Those who seek beauty must not pose it as an external object of vision, but merge their identity with it.[62] What kind of vision could this be?

59. 4.6 [41].1.37–41.
60. 4.6 [41].2.1–9.
61. 2.4 [12].5.6–13.
62. 5.8 [31].10.35–44.

Plotinus answers: "If he sees it as something different, he is not yet in beauty, but he is in it most perfectly when he becomes it. If therefore sight is of something external we must not have sight, or only that which is identical with its object. This is a sort of intimate understanding and perception of a self which is careful not to depart from itself by wanting to perceive too much" (5.8 [31].11.20–24). Again, the object is regarded from the perspective not of the percipient but of the thing seen.

The art historian André Grabar finds in these passages a deep affinity with the plastic art of late antiquity.[63] There is in that tradition a tendency to resist perspective. Everything is reduced to one plane surface in which each object may be seen (on Plotinus' theory) in its true size and detail. There is even sometimes a deliberate reversal of perspective, as if to emphasize the point. Often the objects are depicted as if irradiated from one in the centre, so that they are seen not in relation to the percipient but in relation to the central object. The object's luminosity is thereby emphasized as if to stress its self-manifestation.

Plotinian optics makes each particular object of vision something of intrinsic value. It does not derive its worth simply as a function of my perspective on the universe. Nor is it ever absorbed into or plundered of its unity and identity by other things. Its relationship is to a whole of which the percipient himself is a sentient part rather than an objective or alien observer. We have said that Form is for Plotinus an intrinsically valuable object of spiritual or intellective vision. We may now also see that it is a subject of such experience. Indeed, in Intellect, our distinction between subject and object breaks down. For Plotinus all things contemplate.[64] Thus Plotinus does not pursue the chimera of objectivity in the sensible world either. The particular, like the Form of which it is an icon, is, both as seer and as seen, of intrinsic value.

---

63. Grabar, "Plotin et les origines," 15–29.
64. 3.8 [30].5.30.

II

Light

PLOTINUS BORROWS many figures from sensible experience to describe the intelligible world, most of which need considerable qualification to avoid suggesting the conflation of intelligible with sensible reality. For example, Plotinus compares the presence of intelligible reality to the sensible world to the force exerted by a hand upon a plank.[1] The hand exerts this power without being divided among the various parts of the plank. In this way the "day and sail" argument of Plato's *Parmenides* is to be overcome.[2] Form is not, by its presence, divided among the particulars. It is to the force exerted by the hand, not to the hand itself, that comparison is made. The hand itself, as it is corporeal and hence divisible, must be figuratively qualified as "incorporeal" if it is to be useful as an image of presence. Plotinus proceeds to qualify this imagery by juxtaposing imagery of the presence of light. The source of light has light not *qua* body, but *qua* luminous body, for light is incorporeal.[3]

The most adequate of all the sensible figures employed by Plotinus to describe intelligible reality is light. Plotinus believes that sensible light is incorporeal. For this reason, unlike the hand, it needs no further qualification to reveal its incorporeality. It already shares incorporeality with Form. Light may also be wholly present to a plurality of objects without being divided among them.

Light is also in an immediate, dynamic, and continuous relationship

1. 6.4 [22].7.
2. 130e4–131e7.
3. For an examination of this passage in the light of the "day and sail" argument of the *Parmenides*, see Schroeder, "The Platonic *Parmenides*," 52–53.

with its source. The source has only to be and to remain what it is for light to proceed from it. In the previous chapter, we saw that Form is for Plotinus an intrinsically valuable object of intellective and spiritual vision and enjoyment, apart from its uses for causation and explanation. However, Plotinus is not content with a disjunction between Form as an intrinsically valuable object of intellective and spiritual vision and enjoyment, and as a cause or explanation. He wishes to build the intrinsic value of the Form, apart from use and explanation, into the structure of creation itself. The sensible world should be utterly dependent upon the intelligible world for its existence, with no need for mediation between them. Thus the Form does not derive its value from its being a pattern on the basis of which other things are made or understood. The reverse is true. It is by being what it is in its intrinsic nature, without mediation, that it both creates and explains all that proceeds from it as its image. The questions of its being and of its relationship to the world will not ultimately admit of separation.

The image of light allows Plotinus to accomplish this purpose, since for him light is an effect of the source alone, while, and indeed because, the source remains what it is in undiminished giving. Reflection fulfills the conditions of illumination. A luminous object may, as source of light and reflection, appear in a mirror. The image in the mirror is the effect only of the source. When the subject of the reflection retires, the mirror image must vanish, for it depends for its existence on the source alone. On the other hand, the withdrawal of the reflective surface does not diminish the luminosity of the source; it continues to project the image, whether or not there is a surface on which it may appear.

Reflection, as a special case of illumination, makes a vital contribution to its figurative uses. If the luminous source is pure light, it projects an image of itself – light – that is, like itself, luminous (although in lesser degree or intensity). Reflection of light, colour, and shape yields a more complex image. That rich image differs from the kind that we find in artistic representation, for the artistic image is not ontically dependent upon its subject in the same way as is the reflected image. Moreover, the characteristics of the luminous original are, in reflection, not merely represented in the mirror (as the characteristics of the original are on the canvas), but truly present.

When an author makes significant use of something in figurative language, it is surely worthwhile to examine what he understands by that thing as it is in itself, apart from its illustrative uses. It must then be legitimate to explore the Plotinian physics of light. The text below deals with this and also yields abundant insight into the Plotinian physics of reflection, since Plotinus sees reflection as an instance of illumination. Reflection (as in a mirror) is, like illumination, used figuratively by Plotinus. Let us now return to the text which we considered at the beginning of the first chapter, 4.5 [29].7. [4]

Plotinus says of light:

The light from luminous bodies, therefore, is the external activity (ἐνέργεια) of a luminous body; but the light in bodies of this kind, bodies, that is, that are primarily and originally of this kind, is altogether substance, corresponding to the form of the primarily luminous body. When a body of this kind together with its matter enters into a mixture, it gives colour; but the activity by itself does not give colour, but only, so to speak, tints the surface, since it belongs to something else and is, one might say, dependent on it, and what separates itself from this something else separates itself from its activity. But one must consider light as altogether incorporeal, even if it belongs to a body. Therefore "it has gone away" (ἀπελήλυθε) or "it is present" (πάρεστιν) are not used of it in their proper sense, but in a different way, and its real existence is an activity. For the image in a mirror must also be called an activity: that which is reflected in it acts on what is capable of being affected without flowing into it; but if the object reflected is there (πάρεστι), the reflection too appears in the mirror and it exists as an image of a coloured surface shaped in a particular way; and if the object goes away (ἀπέλθῃ), the mirror-surface no longer has what it had before, when the object seen in it offered itself to it for its activity. (4.5 [29].7.33–49)[5]

We may first observe that light is, for Plotinus, incorporeal, even if it proceeds from a bodily source. In accepting the incorporeality of light, Plotinus agrees with Aristotle who says of light in the *De Anima* that it is "neither fire nor corporeal at all, nor an emanation from any body (for it would in that case be a kind of body), but the presence (παρουσία) of fire or something of that nature in the transparent."[6] It is unclear what Aristotle understands here by "presence." The ᴧ ᵣ

---

4. p. 3.
5. My translation.
6. ii.7.418b9–10.

istotelian Alexander of Aphrodisias, who was read in Plotinus' seminar,[7] seeks to clarify this.

Colour comes about in the illumined and in light, just as light in the transparent, not like some emanation, nor because matter or the transparent receive the light or the colour of light. If the sources of these are removed, immediately colour is gone from the transparent (if the sources which colour light depart [ἀπελθόντων]) and light is also gone from the transparent (if that which illumines it is not present [παρείη]). Rather there is change from both [both sources of colour and light and coloured or illumined objects] in those things [i.e., light in the case of colour and the transparent in the case of light] that receive them [i.e., colour and light] in accordance with presence and the character of their relation (κατὰ παρουσίαν τε καὶ ποιὰν σχέσιν), as is the case of objects that are seen in mirrors. As I have said, the illumined are transparent in actuality. When there is something in them which is capable of being transparent and this is in actuality, then they are eminently and in act transparent, when they receive their perfection and their native form *qua* transparent from the light. For light is the act and perfection of the transparent *qua* transparent. This light comes about in the transparent by the presence of fire or the divine body. For light comes about in accordance with the relation of that which is able to illumine to those objects which are capable of being illumined. For light is not a body. (*De Anima* 42.19–43.)[8]

Clearly Alexander is faithful to Aristotle in his insistence that light is not corporeal. Plotinus certainly agrees on this point but corrects Alexander in his account of the genesis of illumination. For Alexander, illumination is an artifact of the spatial relation or juxtaposition of the source of light and the illuminated object. When the ingredients of illumination depart (ἀπελθόντων) or are no longer present (παρείη), the illumination ceases. He offers the example of reflection in a mirror. When the subject of the reflection and the mirror are juxtaposed, then reflection takes place. When they are removed from each other, reflection ceases.

Where Alexander (following Aristotle) sees light as the actualization of the diaphanous medium,[9] Plotinus sees it as the activity of the

7. Porphyry *Vita Plotini* 14.13.

8. Ed. I Bruns, *Alexandri Aphrodisiensis praeter commentaria scripta minora: de Anima liber cum Mantissa.* (*Supplementum Aristotelicum* ii.1 [Berlin 1887]). My translation.

9. *De Anima* ii.7.418b9–10.

source of illumination directed externally. Plotinus regards the language of spatiotemporal presence and departure as, strictly speaking, inappropriate to the discussion of light, which is incorporeal. He thus confines the use of the verb "be present" (παρεῖναι) and "depart" (ἀπέρχεσθαι) to the source.[10]

Plotinus and Alexander also differ over the role played by the source of illumination. For Alexander, the source of light is a cause that can produce illumination only in concert with the object to be illuminated. For Plotinus, the source of light is the unique cause of illumination. This difference recurs in their accounts of reflection.[11]

We saw, at the beginning of the first chapter, that Plotinus uses the metaphysical example of the procession of soul from soul to illustrate the physics of light. Let us re-examine this comparison. Plotinus has just argued that the source of light is on its own the cause of illumination. If the luminous subject is withdrawn from the mirror, its reflection will not appear. Now Plotinus appeals to his model: "But with soul also, in so far as it is an activity of another prior soul, as long as the higher soul abides (μενούσης), so does the dependent activity" (4.5 [29].7.49–51).[12] The word "abide" (μένειν) is obviously appropriate to illumination.[13] As long as the source of light abides, the light will proceed from that source in undiminished giving.

"Abiding" is employed to describe how the One, in its production of Intellect, remains unchanged:

When, therefore, the Intelligible "abides (μένοντος) in its own way of life," that which comes into being does come into being from it, but from it as it abides unchanged. Since, therefore, it abides as Intelligible, what comes into being does so as thinking: and since it is thinking and thinks that from which it came – for it has nothing else – it becomes Intellect, like another intelligible and like that Principle, a representation and image of it. But how, when that abides unchanged, does Intellect come into being? In each and every thing

10. 4.5 [29].7.42.

11. On illumination and reflection Alexander and Plotinus, see Schroeder, "Analogy of the Active Intellect to Light" and "Light and the Active Intellect in Alexander and Plotinus;" further discussion of illumination in Alexander and Plotinus will be found in Schroeder and Todd, *Two Greek Aristotelian Commentators*, 14–19.

12. Trans. Armstrong (slightly modified to render μένειν "abide," rather than "remain").

13. Cf. 4.3 [27].17.18.

there is an activity which belongs to substance and one which goes out from substance (ἐνέργεια ἡ μὲν ἐστι τῆς οὐσίας, ἡ δὲ ἐκ τῆς οὐσίας ἑκάστου); and that which belongs to substance is the active actuality which is each particular thing, and the other activity derives from that first one, and must in everything be a consequence of it, different from the thing itself: as in fire there is a heat which is the content of its substance, and another which comes into being from that primary heat when fire exercises the activity which is native to its substance in abiding unchanged as fire. So it is also in the higher world; and much more so there, while the Principle "abides in its own proper way of life," the activity generated from the perfection in it and its coexistent activity acquires substantial experience, since it comes from a great power (δυνάμεως), the greatest indeed of all, and arrives at being and substance. (5.4 [7].2.22–37)

As the flame, just by being what it is, issues in heat, so does the One, simply by being what it is, give rise to Intellect and all of its sequents. Indeed this pattern is extended universally as Plotinus argues that in each and every thing that is there is one activity that inheres in its substance and another that proceeds from its substance. Obviously, the source of light and light would provide the paradigm. The verb "abide" (μένειν), which is used of the One in this passage, may also be used of the source of light in illumination, as we have seen. This verb well illustrates the intransitive activity of the source that, while remaining or abiding what it is, gives rise to a transitive activity that proceeds from it.

"Abiding" may then appropriately describe the intransitive activity of the source of light. The use of the term in this passage owes a literary debt to Plato's *Timaeus*. Plotinus says that the One "abides" as what it is in its act of creation, even as the flame abides or remains what it is and, simply by being what it is, produces heat. In the *Timaeus* Plato says that the Demiurge "abided in his own way of life" (ἔμενεν ἐν τῷ ἑαυτοῦ κατὰ τρόπον ἤθει) after his creation of soul and before he left the creation of mortal bodies to his children.[14] Plato proceeds to say that, while the Demiurge was "abiding" (μένοντος), his children thought to obey their father. Plotinus resumes this use of the participle as he describes the abiding of the One (lines 21–22): μένοντος αὐτοῦ ἐν τῷ οἰκείῳ ἤθει ("when – the Intelligible [the One as intelligible

14. 42e5–6.

object] 'abides in its own proper way of life'"). The phrase is resumed at lines 33–34: "While the Principle 'abides in its own proper way of life.'" The significance of this appeal to the authority of Plato will be discussed later.

The procession of heat from a flame is offered as a specific example of a general principle that in everything that is there is both an intransitive activity and a transitive activity that proceeds from it and is dependent upon it. It is apparent that the procession of light from a luminous source, heat from flame, and Intellect from the One all exemplify this principle. To understand this principle more clearly, it is helpful to review an aspect of Plotinus' doctrine of potency and act. Among the meanings of potency (*dunamis*) Aristotle includes both the power to act and the capacity to be acted upon.[15] Plotinus does use this term in the latter sense.[16] It is, however, the sense of power to act that is relevant to the present discussion.[17]

Plotinus argues that a *dunamis* in the sense of power to act will produce from itself an activity (*energeia*). Thus the *dunamis* of courage (ἀνδρία) produces the activity (*energeia*) of courageous behaviour (τὸ ἀνδρίζεσθαι).[18] It is in this active sense of *dunamis* that the One is said to be the might or power that creates all things. Plotinus explains: "The One is potency of all things (δύναμις τῶν πάντων). But in what way is it the potency? Not in the way in which matter is said to be in potency, because it receives: for matter is passive; but this [material] way of being a potency is at the opposite extreme to making" (5.3 [49].15.32–35). The creation is the activity produced from that power.[19]

Enneads 6.4 [22] and 6.5 [23], entitled "The Presence of Being Everywhere," are addressed to the problem of how intelligible reality may be present to the sensible world without corruption of its unity and identity. In these writings, Plotinus confronts the kinds of objections raised by Parmenides in the introduction to Plato's *Parmenides*. Plotinus considers that intelligible reality might be present to the sensible

---

15. *Metaphysics* ix.1.1046a.

16. Cf. 2.5 [25].1.17–20 and Buchner, *Plotins Möglichkeitslehre*, 17–20.

17. On the Plotinian uses of the Aristotelian doctrine of act and potency, see further De Gandillac, "Plotin et la 'Métaphysique' d'Aristote."

18. 2.5 [25].2.33–36. Plotinus may be influenced in this by the Stoic use of *dunamis* and by Zeno's argument that a quality is the cause of a predicate: See Schroeder, "Representation and Reflection," 44.

19. 5.3 [49].15.32.

world without sacrifice of its unity and identity if it were present by means of its powers (*dunameis*), and speaks of inferior powers proceeding from higher powers grounded in the substance of the intelligible world.[20]

We may see in this procession the same kind of reasoning that we examined in 5.4 [7].2. There we saw that there is an activity (*energeia*) that inheres in substance and another activity that proceeds from substance. We have also heard Plotinus speak of how an activity (*energeia*) may proceed from a potency or power (*dunamis*). It is obvious that, where *dunamis* is understood in its active sense, the words *dunamis* and *energeia* are interchangeable.

The powers that proceed from the intelligible to the sensible world must then be grounded in the substance of the intelligible world and that substance must not be diminished by their procession. Plotinus enunciates the principle: "Just as it is not possible to have substance without power, so it is not possible to have power without substance" (6.4 [22].9.23–24). So, as the powers proceed from the intelligible world, even though they may, as "light from light" (6.4 [22].9.26–27), be diminished or weakened in comparison with the powers from which they proceed, they are yet yoked to substance in the intelligible world.

Plotinus entertains the objection[21] that an image may continue to exist in the absence of its original. Thus, when the model departs, the portrait remains. In this way the powers which have proceeded from the intelligible world could be cut off from the substance of that world, yet the images of the intelligible world in the world of sense continue.

To disarm this argument, Plotinus distinguishes between two kinds of imitation. In the case of the model and the portrait, the portrait may continue in existence upon the withdrawal of the model. However, in the case of the mirror image, the subject as original creates its image. If the original is withdrawn, the image will vanish. Plotinus appeals to the paradigm not of representation but of reflection in his account of the procession of powers from the intelligible world.[22] Plotinus concludes the chapter by comparing the procession of powers

20. 6.4 [22].9 and 10.
21. 6.4 [22].10.
22. Plotinus rejects (lines 5–11) the argument that, in the case of a self-portrait, the model creates its own image, on the grounds that it is not *qua* model, but *qua* artist that he performs the act.

from the intelligible world to the undiminished giving of light on the part of the sun.[23] We have already seen from 4.5 [29].7 that reflection fulfills the conditions of illumination.

There is then a doctrine in Plotinus that, in the case of everything that is, there is one intransitive activity or power that is at one with its essence and another transitive activity or power that proceeds from the first and yet continues in dynamic continuity with it.[24] This principle is instantiated, as we have seen, in the case of phenomena in the sensible world: source of light and light, reflection, flame and heat. It is also exemplified in metaphysical instances: the procession of soul from soul, of Intellect from the One, and the procession of powers from the intelligible to the sensible world.

We may compare the example of the source of light and light with other examples drawn from the world of sensible objects. Procession of an inferior from a superior entity is illustrated as well by the examples of cold and snow, scent and flower, [25] the stream and spring, or plant and root.[26] As we have observed from 4.5 [29].7, light is incorporeal for Plotinus. The incorporeality of light constitutes a crucial difference from the other figures borrowed from the sensible world. As light is incorporeal, it need not be divided among the objects to which it is present, for, like the "day" in the "day and sail" arguments of the Platonic *Parmenides,* it has no size.[27] Even if the source of light is corporeal, it is not *qua* body that it is luminous, but *qua* luminous body.[28] Basically then we have light from light, a weaker or inferior light, from a stronger or superior light. Indeed, in 6.4 [22].9.26–27, the powers descend from the intelligible world as "light from light" (φῶς ἀπὸ φωτὸς). The procession of sensible light from its source is therefore a more adequate illustration of the procession of one metaphysical entity from another, or of the procession of sensible reality from an incorporeal and intelligible source, than are the other figures of speech borrowed from the world of sense experience.

Light exists in a relation of dynamic continuity with its source. In this way too, it is an adequate image of such procession. In so far as

23. 6.4 [22].10.26–30.
24. Cf. Schroeder, "Conversion and Consciousness," 191–92.
25. 5.1 [10].6.35–7.
26. 3.8 [30].10.
27. 6.4 [22].8.
28. 6.4 [22].7.31; cf. 5.5 [32].7.11–14.

other images fulfill this condition, they are similarly adequate. However, as they are corporeal, they are useful only in so far as their corporeality is suspended for the purposes of the analogy. Qualifying them thus also makes them more like the case of illumination. Therefore the image of light is the most adequate to express the nature of intelligible reality and its dynamic and immediate presence. In the next chapter, we shall see that light's diaphanous and self-manifesting character further augments its adequacy as image of intelligible reality.[29]

29. On the theme of the ontological adequacy of images see Beierwaltes, "Metaphysik des Lichtes" and "*Nachwort*." Of all the images used by Plotinus, Beierwaltes sees in light the image that yields the greatest degree of adequacy. Beierwaltes "Metaphysik des Lichtes" and "*Nachwort*" corrects Ferwerda, *Signification des images*, 46 ff. who sees the image of light as only a convenient and imperfect analogy. In the light and sphere analogy of 6.4 [22].7, Plotinus states that the sphere is not illumined because it is a body, for it has light, not *qua* body, but *qua* luminous body, by a power that is not bodily. Later (ibid. 8.1) Plotinus reminds us that the light is from a body. Since Plotinus thus distinguishes between sensible and intelligible light, argues Charrue, *Plotin Lecteur de Platon*, 237–38, then intelligible light is, *pace* Beierwaltes, merely a metaphor based on the model of sensible light. But Beierwaltes is insisting that if anything, whether sensible or intelligible, fulfills the conditions required for there to be light, then it *is* light. Charrue also seems to miss the point, stated so insistently by Plotinus in 6.4 [22].7.29–32, that the fact that light proceeds from a body does not render light corporeal. Blumenthal, "Plotinus in the Light of Scholarship," 542, in agreement with Cilento, "Stile e Linguaggio nella filosofia di Plotino"; Ferwerda, *Signification des images*; and Aubin, "L'image dans l'oeuvre de Plotin," sees figurative language in Plotinus as having no independent value, merely illuminating what is not known by what is. The relationship between original and image in Plotinus' system is one in which the image plays an inferior role. Therefore light is an image like any other. Beierwaltes properly asks us to distinguish degrees of ontological accuracy in figurative language. Barbanti, *La metaphora in Plotino*, 155 note 185, agrees with Ferwerda, *Signification des images*, in rejecting Beierwaltes' position. She offers (79–80) Plotinus' denial that light may be said either to be present or to depart (4.5 [29].7.42 – see my argument above, pp. 25–28) as a qualification of the metaphor of light that just illustrates the approximate character of metaphor in general. On the contrary, Plotinus is stating what are in fact the properties of light! Fielder, "Plotinus' Copy Theory," 6 (who does not engage Beierwaltes) remarks with perspicacity (of 6.4 [22].7): "Light is more than just a metaphor, it is almost an instance of how intelligible reality generates its extended image." Pelikan, *Light of the World*, 33–34 sees in Athanasius the same view and usage of light imagery that Beierwaltes and I see in Plotinus: "At one level of discourse it was accurate to say that the statement 'God is light' was symbolic. Yet this did not mean that one already knew, from some source or other apart from God, what light was, and that one attributed some quality of this light to God. On the contrary, God was uncreated light, the light that illumined every other light, himself the ultimate source of every illumination in the universe."

The images of spring and stream, snow and cold, flower and scent, etc. suggest to a reader with even the most casual acquaintance with Plotinus the notion of "emanation." Undiminished giving on the part of the divine is described as a flowing forth, or an overflow, from a superior and inexhaustible source. Usually the images regarded as illustrating "emanation" are taken to have a rude equality for this purpose. However, they need to be cleared of vulgar material associations eventually. The word "emanation" has been much abused and done a great disservice to our author. How convenient this word is for the tired historian of philosophy who can use it to discharge his task by providing a tedious and alienating account of Plotinus' "system," a weird contraption of descending goo and ascending vapours! The necessary qualifications that the imagery requires can be as dreary as "emanation" itself.

In fact, "emanation" is not a term fondly embraced by Plotinus. Aristotle specifically denies that light is an emanation (ἀπορροή).[30] Alexander also denies this (οὔτε κατὰ ἀπόρροιαν τινα)[31] as does Plotinus (οὐ ῥέοντος).[32] We shall see that the various images other than light, such as fire and heat, snow and cold, spring and stream, should be qualified in the direction of and understood in terms of the ontologically adequate image of light.

Thus Plotinus says of the procession of Intellect from the One:

How did it come to be then, and what are we to think of as surrounding the One in its repose? It must be a radiation from it while it abides (μένοντος) unchanged, like the bright light of the sun which, so to speak, runs round it, springing from it continually while it abides unchanged. All things which exist, as long as they abide (μένει) in being, necessarily produce from their own substances, in dependence on their present power, a surrounding reality directed to what is outside them, a kind of image of the archetypes from which it was produced: fire produces the heat which comes from it; snow does not only keep its cold inside itself. Perfumed things show this particularly clearly. As long as they exist, something is diffused from themselves around them, and what is near them enjoys their existence. (5.1 [10].6.27–37)[33]

30. *De Anima* II.7.418b15.

31. *De Anima* 42.20–21.

32. 4.5 [29].7.46.

33. Trans. Armstrong (slightly modified; I have for my purposes preferred to render μένειν with "abide" rather than "remain.") It should be clear from my argument that I attach more colour to this word than do most scholars.

The irradiation of light and the procession of heat from fire, cold from snow, and scent from flower instantiate the general principle that all beings, as they abide (μένειν) as what they are, produce an image outside themselves. The procession of light from its source, in contrast with these other images, provides the only ontologically adequate image for creation. The other images need to be qualified and refined so that they may be truly useful. They need to be qualified in the direction of attaining precisely the adequacy which light already possesses, e.g., the incorporeality of light not only represents but also shares the incorporeality of the entities which Plotinus means to discuss. Unlike light, that is already incorporeal, the corporeal character of the source must be suspended if the image is to express the production of a corporeal world from an incorporeal source. In fact, Plotinus polemicizes against the language of emanation.[34] "Emanation" imagery succeeds, on the other hand, to the extent that it expresses the relation of dynamic continuity that exists between light and its source.

We have seen how, in 4.5 [29].7.49–51, Plotinus, to illustrate the physics of light, scandalously invokes the metaphysical image of the procession of soul from soul. In the first chapter,[35] it was remarked that this use of metaphysics toward the understanding of physics demonstrates Plotinus' primary orientation toward the intelligible world. We should now be in a position to offer a closer interpretation of this passage. If light and its source are both incorporeal and stand to each other in a relation of dynamic continuity, then sensible light need not be light *proprio sensu*. Anything else that fulfills these two conditions *is* light.

Perhaps we should not be so very surprised by Plotinus' use in 4.5 [29].7.49–51 of a metaphysical example to describe a phenomenon of physics. If light is the most adequate image that illustrates the nature of the intelligible world, not just by analogy, but by its ontological correspondence, e.g., incorporeality, then surely a phenomenon of the intelligible world may, in a proper observation of parity, be employed to illustrate the nature of light. After all, we are in each case proceeding from the term of comparison to the *tertium comparationis*.

34. Cf. 5.1 [10].3.10–12; 2.1 [40].8.3–4 and Dörrie, "Emanation," 135–37 (83–85 in reprint in *Platonica Minora*); cf. further Beierwaltes, *Ewigkeit und Zeit*, 18; *Platonismus und Idealismus*, 120–1; Armstrong, "Plotinus," 239–41.

35. pp. 3–4.

We have observed how the words "abide" and "abiding" (μένειν) are used to describe the way in which the source of illumination, sensible or intelligible, remains what it is while light proceeds from it as transitive expression of an intransitive activity or power, at one with its essence. We have also interpreted such abiding on the part of the One (in the production of Intellect) by reference to Plato's *Timaeus*.[36] In the Platonic passage, the Demiurge "abided in his own way of life" after he had created soul and left the fashioning of mortal bodies to his children. This "abiding" on the part of the Demiurge is equated by Plotinus with abiding on the part of the luminous source in creation (e.g., the One in the production of Intellect).

Plato's account in the *Timaeus* of the creation of the world by a divine Demiurge or craftsman was the subject of controversy in antiquity. According to Aristotle, followed by his school and by Plutarch, the story was to be interpreted literally and hence creation took place in time. Xenocrates, Crantor, and the philosophers of the Platonic Academy interpreted this creation story as an allegory and regarded the world as eternal.[37]

Plotinus certainly does not accept that a maker of the universe should literally have hands or feet, or literally exercise deliberative thought.[38] He obviously discards any vulgar literal understanding of creation. Even taken allegorically, there is something very basic to this account of creation that troubles him deeply. The story implies some kind of mediation between intelligible and sensible reality, even if literally there is no figure such as the Demiurge who would perform this function. Such mediation, as it employs the Form as an instrument of production, tends to obscure its intrinsic value.

36. Cf. 5.4 [7].2.21–22; ibid. 33–34 and Plato *Timaeus* 42e5–6; cf. 5.4 [7].2.26 for the application of μένειν to the abiding of the One in its consubstantial and intransitive activity; line 34 for abiding on the part of fire in the procession of heat.

37. The evidence is presented in Frutiger, *Les Mythes de Platon*, 200, note 1; cf. Robinson, *Plato's Psychology*, 61–62, 62 note 12. The two positions are exemplified in Proclus, *In Timaeum* 89b (Diehl I 290/30–291/3), for whom the world is eternal and Plutarch, *De animae procreatione* 1016cd, for whom the world was created in time.

38. The qualification of deliberative thought and activity on the part of the Platonic creator doubtless arises from the internal requirements of Plotinus' own position; however, it may also be situated within Plotinus' polemic against the Gnostics, cf. 5.8 [31].7.2–12; 5.8 [31].12.20–22 and Hadot, "Structure et Thèmes," 643; 648; cf. 2.9 [33].4.6–7 and Sinnige, "Gnostic influences," 90: there is no Gnostic "gliding down" (νεῦσις) of the Soul in its act of creation which is rather an illumination which proceeds from the Soul which abides what it is.

To the end of establishing the intrinsic value of Form, Plotinus supplements the model of representation with another paradigm, that of reflection.[39] He distinguishes between an image that exists by nature and an image that exists by art or craft. In the case of the image that exists by art, the image once accomplished may exist in the absence of its original. Reflection in any reflective surface yields the image that exists by nature. With no artistic intervention, the autumnal maple tree is reflected in our Canadian lakes. The subject of the reflection, the tree, itself creates the image upon the surface of the water. This reflection involves no act of making, not even an act of deliberation or discursive thought on the part of the tree. Indeed, it seems to require no act or deed of hand or mind for its realization. The tree has simply to be where it is rooted for the lovely image to occur. Being, in this instance, is prior to any productive event, although it does not preclude production. Indeed, the pattern or model may not be discarded once the image is produced. The model of reflection thus eliminates the need for mediation of the kind provided by representation.

The model of artistic representation has nevertheless valuable uses for the philosopher. When we invoke the Form as cause or explanation, we need to specify the relation between the Form and the particulars. If we specify it in terms of "participation," we encounter the danger of seeing the Form as corporeal and divisible. If we specify it in terms of "likeness," we risk confusing pattern with copy.

To overcome these misunderstandings, the philosopher must reexamine participation and likeness and describe them in such a way that confusion of Form with particulars is avoided. Thus if the Form is originally defined as immaterial, the unity and identity of the Form will not be compromised by participation. Through careful distinction between attributes of similarity and attributes of imitation, confusion of the original and the image may be avoided. The model of artistic representation separates the intelligible and sensible realms as the subject of a painting is separate from the painted image. (Such separation is not to be found in the model of reflection). That separation facilitates discursive comparison of the model and the image. So what it loses in concealing the dynamic continuity of image with original, it gains in making appropriate distinctions between them.

39. For the distinction, see Schroeder, "Representation and Reflection."

In this act of explaining the relationship between Form and the particulars, the philosopher, as it were, occupies a space between them, looking now in the direction of Form and then in the direction of the particulars in pursuit of an objective account which will not confuse these two realities. An artist represents his subject by dividing it into a multiplicity of attributes of similarity that, in their quasi-unity, present an image in division of the original. We may refer to this kind of exposition, where it follows this analogy, as "representation." Of course, it is true that the distance presupposed by this form of exposition is useful to the philosopher in understanding the relationship between the Form and the particulars. It is also true that the very act of demonstrating that the particular is an image of a higher reality may perform the anagogical function of inviting us to seek the Form. Nevertheless it eclipses the intrinsic value of the Form to the extent that it is viewed only from the horizon of the particular whose existence it is invoked to explain. As we have seen, Plotinus wishes to build the intrinsic value of the Form, apart from use and explanation, into the structure of creation itself. The model of representation must be supplemented by the model of reflection. We are not to consider the being of Form apart from the question of its relationship to the particulars, for its being is such that the particulars are ontically dependent upon it.

In the case of visible reflection, the natural image may exhibit a great difference from the image of art or representation. The artist may represent the colour blue in his subject's eye by means of a daub of blue paint. In the case of the reflected image, light and colour from the subject's eye actually produces light and colour in the image. We have here, not mere representation, but the real presence of an attribute of the subject in the image. We have, in the place of artistic distance, the immediacy of dynamic continuity. Yet that relationship is constituted, not by any relational act, but simply by the subject abiding in its own being, which is not plundered by its relationships to other things.

Thus the sovereignty of the One in the creation inheres not in its relationship to the creation, but in the creation's being an immediate consequence of the One's being what it is, i.e., it is derived from the One's intrinsic value. In the case of every being in the Plotinian universe, "that" absorbs "why," the act of being precedes and subsumes all instrumentality.

The relationship of pattern and copy, with its mediating Demiurge, is then only one model of the relationship between image and original. Another model is offered by reflection. The artist represents the blue in his subject's eyes by means of a daub of blue paint. If that same subject stands before a mirror, the blue in the subject's eyes is reflected in the mirror. As the light and colour in the subject's eyes proceed immediately and continuously from the eyes to the reflective surface, we may say that the colour blue which is in the eyes of the subject is *truly* present, not merely represented, in the mirror image. Thus in 6.4 [22].10, the powers proceed from the intelligible world to the image in the world of sense and remain in dynamic continuity with their source. It belongs to the realism of Plotinus that he wishes to supplement, indeed correct, the otherwise useful model of representation with one of reflection. Of course, the image in representation and the image in reflection share in common that they divide the original into attributes of similarity. In the reflected image the various attributes *qua* expressed in that image do not inhere in the unity and substance of the original, any more than they do in the image of representation, even though they are not the product of discursive analysis and are severally in dynamic continuity with the attributes of the original. Nevertheless the image in reflection contains such attributes in real presence.

III

Silence

THE WORLD AS reflected image is, in contrast to the product of art or craft, begotten, not made. By employing the notion of begetting, Plotinus suggests that in the case of the world the relationship between creator and created is immediate: there is no mediator (e.g., Demiurge) between them. In begetting, we produce from ourselves. The act requires no deliberate address to pattern, copy, and material, as production by artisan or artist.

We shall see that Plotinus supplements the language of begetting with words referring to silence as he portrays creation. Ultimately, this vocabulary of silence is justified by his account of reflection. On his view, a surface must be calm or silent before it can reflect. A noble scene in nature may reflect the world of Form. It may also make us reflective. As the human mind surveys natural beauty, it may address, not only the scene before it, but, in and through it, the intelligible original or Form of which nature is a reflection. The human mind may, as may nature, be said to reflect the Form. Such reflection may mark the beginning of our return to the world of Form.

We also say that the subject before a mirror is reflected in the mirror. That subject need do nothing but be itself, nothing but abide, in order to be reflected, in order that that the transitive act of light and reflection be manifested in the mirror. The calm or silence of the reflective surface is here matched by the calm or silence of the luminous and reflective source.

Let us begin our study of silence in Plotinus by exploring the image of begetting and its relationship to silence.[1] We have seen that Plotinus

1. The present study of silence in Plotinus rests in part on Schroeder, "Representation and Reflection," in which further bibliography on this subject may be found.

employs the language of "abiding" and "reflection" so that he may interpret the creation story of the *Timaeus* in terms of dynamic continuity and immediacy. He also tries to avoid suggesting that the demiurgic power must be an agent external to pattern and copy by employing the imagery of "begetting" (γεννᾶν) rather than "making" (ποιεῖν). At *Timaeus* 28c3–4, Plato calls the Demiurge "creator and father of this universe" (ποιητὴν καὶ πατέρα τοῦδε τοῦ παντός).[2] Plotinus sees the words "and father" as epexegetic of the word "creator," so that he may interpret the creation as an act of begetting, rather than of craftsmanship. Each reality begets from itself that which is below it.[3] The relationship of father who begets and son who is begotten prevails throughout the Plotinian universe. The One is Ouranos; the Intellect, Kronos; the Soul, Zeus.[4] Plotinus observes: "Intellect therefore makes soul more divine by its being father and by being present to it (ποιεῖ καὶ τῷ πατὴρ εἶναι καὶ τῷ παρεῖναι); for there is nothing between them but the fact that they are different" (5.1 [10].3.20–22). The notion of begetting, of the relationship between father and son, is here invoked to suggest immediacy. Presence requires no agent, external to Intellect and the Soul, that would mediate between them. In a wonderful play on words, Plotinus sees "be present" (παρεῖναι) as a contraction of "being father" (πατὴρ εἶναι). The passage is also alliterative, as the words "make," "father," and "be present" all begin with the same letter. Plotinus intends that we see here a semantic triad of creating, begetting, and presence.

We may see in the Plotinian attribution of "begetting" to the intelligible world a response to Aristotle's argument against the Platonic theory of Forms that the Form cannot be the cause of genesis. Aristotle argues that one man begets another, a Peleus an Achilles; it is not the Form of Man which begets man.[5] Plotinus, by contrast, sees begetting precisely as a great cosmic principle of creation in which the creation of man must also, ultimately, be embraced.

2. At *Timaeus* 37c7 the Demiurge is described as the "father who begat;" cf. *Politicus* 273b1–2.

3. Cf. 5.1 [10].6.37–50.

4. 3.8 [30].11.33–45; 5.8 [31].12.3–13.11. The story of Ouranos, Kronos, and Zeus is told by Hesiod *Theogony* 154–210 and reported by Plato in *Republic* 377e6–378a6. The latter abominated the myth and said it should be confined to an esoteric circle of initiates. Plotinus takes him at his word, cf. Hadot, "Ouranos, Kronos, and Zeus;" Pépin, *Mythe et Allégorie*, 203–6.

5. *Metaphysics* vii.8.1033b16–1034a8; ix.8.1049b24–27; x.4.1070b30–35; x.5. 1071a20–24.

Aristotle argues that, if the Platonic Form is separate from the particulars, it cannot be the cause for them of their being.[6] Plotinus employs the language of begetting, of the closeness in love of father and son, to respond to this objection. Thus the Intellect looks to the One,

> But it sees him, not as separated from him, but because it comes next after him, and there is nothing between, as also there is nothing between soul and Intellect. Everything longs for its parent and loves it, especially when parent and offspring are alone; but when the parent is the highest good, the offspring is necessarily with him and separate from him only in otherness. But we say that Intellect is an image of that Good. (5.1 [10].6.48 – 5.1 [10].7.1)[7]

The relation of original and image is seen in the light of family resemblance, but also in terms of filial appropriation of the paternal model in imitation.

Plotinus brings to crystallization the themes of imitation, begetting, abiding, and reflection as he opposes these to a conception of the Demiurge as an external agent of creation. Soul as Zeus is born from Intellect (sc. Kronos) and thus derives his resemblance to his father.[8] The begetting is described as follows:

> This image imitates its archetype in every way: for it has life and what belongs to reality as a representation of it should, and it has its being beauty since it comes from that higher beauty; and it has its everlastingness in the way proper to an image; otherwise [the intelligible universe] will sometimes have an image and sometimes not – and this image is not the product of art (τέχνη), but every natural image (φύσει εἴκων) exists as long as its archetype abides (μένει). (5.8 [31].12.15–20)[9]

Notice here the opposition of nature (φύσις) and art or craft (τέχνη). Plotinus clearly sees an image in reflection as a natural image, as opposed to an image as a product of art or craft. The sense of the natural is enriched by the semantic context of begetting.

---

6. *Metaphysics* i.9.991b1–3.
7. Cf. 5.1 [10].3.20–22, which we have just discussed above.
8. 5.8 [31].12.7–11.
9. Trans. Armstrong (slightly modified to render μένειν as "abide," rather than "is there").

We have seen how the source "abides" (μένει) in the act of creation on the model of light and reflection. This abiding of the source is meant to offer an alternative to the model of representation and any making on the part of the Demiurge as craftsman or artist who busily intervenes between the pattern and the copy. The language of "abiding" is joined with the language of silence or quiet (ἡσυχία, σιώπη) to bring out the absence of such behaviour. Thus the source may "abide in silence" in its own innate act; it may simply remain what it is and from its own being the activity of creation will effortlessly and silently proceed. The language of silence and abiding is also used to describe how the source may create without losing its unity and identity in division among its products.

Let us then examine some texts in which "abiding" and "silence" are joined. Plotinus argues that if aspiration to the Good is good, then the Good can have nothing outside itself to which it might aspire:

So if the aspiration and activity toward the best is good, the Good must not look or aspire to something else, but stay quiet (ἐν ἡσύχῳ) and be the "spring and origin"[10] of natural activities, and give other things the form of good, not by its activity directed to them – for they are directed to it, their source. It must not be the Good of activity or thought, but by reason of its very abiding (αὐτῇ τῇ μονῇ). (1.7 [54].1.13–19)[11]

Here Plotinus brings the language of "silence" and "abiding" together to assert the sovereignty of the Good that is good in itself, not simply "good for" something else, e.g., for producing good things. In this context Plotinus is careful to avoid all notion of a Demiurge as an agent external to creator and creation.

A successful immanent interpretation of the Plotinian text will establish a semantic field or fields in which various words are shown to bear an organic relation to each other. This text is the product of long reflection upon and deep internalization of what Plotinus understands as the great motifs and possibilities of Platonic thinking. In interpreting the creation story of the *Timaeus* in terms of "reflection," he uses a genetically related vocabulary, whose terms will function synergistically in passage after passage to assert the sovereignty of

10. The reference is to Plato *Phaedrus* 245c9.
11. With H-S I accept the emendation of μόνη το μονῇ in line 18; a dative is wanted to parallel ἐνεργείᾳ and νοήσει on the same line.

Form and its independence from artificial mediation. A good example of a Plotinian semantic field is presented by 6.9 [9].9 where the terms "light," "abiding," "begetting," and "silence," all of which are associated with the model of reflection, work together. Here Plotinus describes the dance of creation about the One:

In this dance [the Soul] sees the source of life, the source of Intellect, the principle of being, the cause of goodness, the root of the soul; these [products] do not emanate from it, then diminish it; for [they are] not [corporeal] mass; for thus the things begotten (τὰ γεννώμενα) would be perishable. But as it is, they are eternal, because their principle abides (μένει) the same, not divided among them, but abiding whole. For this reason, they also abide, as, if the sun shines, the light also abides. For we are not cut off, nor are we separate. (lines 1–8)[12]

Plotinus further says, of the soul in union with the One (lines 18–19), that it "begets gods in silence (γεννᾷ θεοὺς ἐν ἡσύχῳ), it begets justice, begets virtue." The soul, which takes its rest in the One, enters into the condition of abiding, light, and silence that properly belongs to the One. By so doing, it must also participate in the creation as, with the One, it creates all that follows. Hence the begetting by the One belongs to silence. The emphasis of this passage is on preserving the unity and identity of the One from division among its products. It also seeks to overcome the charge that the Platonic Form is either separate from the particulars and thus cannot contribute to their being or lost in division among them.

Plotinus specifically associates silence or quiet with the absence of the detachment and deliberative thought of the craftsman. Thus he argues:

For it [the All] was the first, and had much power, indeed all power; and this is the power to produce something else without seeking to produce it. For if it had sought, it would not have had it of itself, nor would it have been of its own substance, but it would have been like a craftsman (τεχνίτης) who does not have that ability to produce from himself, but as something acquired, and gets it from learning. So Intellect, by giving something of itself to matter, made all things in unperturbed quietness (ἥσυχος τὰ πάντα εἰργάζετο). (3.2 [47].2.10–16)

12. My translation.

In *Ennead* 3.8 [10], "On Nature, Contemplation and the One," Plotinus describes how Nature creates without levers, without the activity of the wax-maker, without any activity reminiscent of our technology. Nature creates by abiding (μένων ποεῖ)[13] and it produces from a contemplation that abides (θεωρίας μενούσης).[14] Its product is an artifact of Nature observing silence (σιωπώσης).[15] It has its contemplation within itself being silent (ἡσυχῇ) and it is thus that it realizes its product.[16] All proceeds without noise[17] (Ἀψοφητὶ μὲν δὴ πάντα). In the resounding anagogical conclusion of 3.8 [30], we ascend far above Nature to the One, which creates "abiding in silence" (μένουσαν...ἡσύχως).[18]

We have seen that the language of "abiding," "silence" and "light" is used to describe the effortless creation by the One, an act of creation that inheres in the very essence of the One, in which the source is not divided among its effects. This same complex of vocabulary is employed prescriptively. If we abide in silence, we may know the One and return to the condition of our source, a light that itself abides in silence. Plotinus, after he has described Intellect's vision of the One as the light before all light,[19] offers the following advice for those who would seek the One:

But one should not enquire whence it comes, for there is no "whence": for it does not really come or go away anywhere (οὔτε γὰρ ἔρχεται οὔτε ἄπεισιν) but appears or does not appear. So one must not chase after it, but wait [abide] quietly (ἡσυχῇ μένειν) till it appears, preparing oneself to contemplate it, as the eye awaits [abides] (περιμένει) the rising of the sun; and the sun rising over the horizon ("from Ocean", the poets say) gives itself to the eyes to see. But from where will he of whom the sun is an image rise? What is the horizon which he will mount above when he appears? He will be above Intellect itself which contemplates him. For Intellect will be standing first to its contemplation, looking to nothing but the Beautiful, all turning and giving

13. 3.8 [30].3.2.
14. 3.8 [30].3.17–23.
15. 3.8 [30].4.5, reading (with Coleridge and Dodds and now Henry and Schwyzer) σιωπώσης for the σιώπησις of the MSS, cf. H-S, vol. 3 *Addenda at Textum* 319; accepted by Armstrong, vol. III, 3, note 1.
16. 3.8 [30].4.15–22.
17. 3.8 [30].5.25–26.
18. 3.8 [30].10.7.
19. 5.5 [32].7.

itself up to him, and, motionless and filled somehow with strength, it sees first of all itself become more beautiful, all glittering, because he is near. But he did not come as one expected, but came as one who did not come (ἦλθεν ὡς οὐκ ἐλθών), for he was seen, not as having come, but as being there before all things, and even before Intellect came. (5.5 [32].8.1–16)

It will be recalled that in 4.5 [29].7.42, in his discussion of the physics of illumination, Plotinus specifically denies the applicability of spatio-temporal imagery to the incorporeal source of light.[20] Thus it is wrong to say "it has departed" (ἀπελήλυθε) or even that "it is present" (πά-ρεστι). Here Plotinus denies that the light that is the One either comes or departs (οὔτε – ἔρχεται οὔτε ἄπεισιν). The One "came as one who did not come." The verb "be present" (παρεῖναι) is used of the One in the sense that it is present before all things, even before the coming of Intellect. Yet in the rest of the passage[21] this use of language is qualified to preclude understanding presence in terms of spatial location.

So we may greet the One, as that which neither comes nor goes but always remains or abides, by ourselves abiding in silence. Quoting Homer,[22] Plotinus offers us a poetic and striking image of this act of quietness or abiding. Just as the eye waits for or abides (περιμένει) the sunrise, so should we abide the appearance of the One. The sun appears over the horizon (ὁρίζοντος) – as the poets say, "from the Ocean." The generic sense of the Greek word "horizon" as that which limits or defines is relevant here. The horizon, the limits with which Intellect hedges the One, will be shattered as the One manifests itself as a light that will not be so defined.[23]

The philosopher scaling the ladder of love in Plato's *Symposium* is assured: "If therefore he should see that [the One], which provides for all, which abiding (μένον) gives and does not receive anything unto itself, then he, abiding (μένων) in the vision of such a principle and enjoying it, being rendered like it, what beauty would he lack?" (1.6 [1].7.25–28).[24] Here again, the "abiding" of the One qualifies the de-

---

20. Cf. pp. 25–28 above.

21. 5.5 [32].8.16–19.

22. *Iliad* vii.421–22.

23. When a person approaches the All with no place to stand whereby he may define or limit himself (ὁριεῖ) and abides (μεῖνας) there, it is then that he may know the All as All (6.5 [23].7.13–17).

24. My translation.

miurgic imagery of the *Timaeus* towards suggestion of undiminished giving on the part of a principle that is creative simply by being what it is. All thought of utility suspended, our abiding in enjoyment returns us to abide with the One.[25]

Supreme beauty abides (μένον) in the temple and does not emerge lest the uninitiated see it (1.6 [1].8.1–3). We may adduce 1.6 [1].7.2–3 where Plotinus says of the Good, "Anyone who has seen it knows what I mean when I say that it is beautiful." The context here is again religious, as Plotinus adapts the language of the ban on revealing the mysteries to his semantic purposes.[26] Thus access to the shrine requires that we abide in silence.[27]

Illumination exemplifies the proper balance between instrumentality and intrinsic value. The source of light is indeed the origin of light that proceeds from itself. Yet it causes that externally projected light simply by being and by abiding in silence as what it is. It is not merely an instrument of creation. When we heed the prescription to abide in silence, to approach the condition of the luminous source of our being, the appropriate relationship between use and intrinsic value is re-established. In this case, we are to think, not of the source of light and the procession of light, but of light first as instrument, then as intrinsically valuable object of our vision.

We see all things, trees, flowers, houses, children at play, icicles or raindrops, by means of light. Yet light itself seldom becomes the theme of our awareness. We might imagine that, if we were sufficiently dull, we might go through life seeing all of the objects about us by means of light, yet never become aware of the light itself. We may alternatively imagine that, if we were to become truly aware of light, everything we see would be seen as a function of light and we might begin a new life in a Rembrandtian universe in which all is light, or seen in terms of light and its absence, shadow.

We have seen how (in 5.5 [32].8) we are enjoined to abide in silence

---

25. There is also a negative sense of abiding, *viz.* clinging to the sensible world, compared with the embrace of the image (to the exclusion of Form) by Narcissus (1.6 [1].8.15) and Odysseus remaining with Kirke (rather than proceeding to his homeland, i.e., the intelligible world [1.6 [1].8.19]).

26. Cf. 6.9 [9].9.46–47. See Pausanias i.37.4 on not revealing why beans are forbidden to initiates in the Eleusinian mysteries and on Orphics as source of the formula, "He who has seen ... knows what I mean." Cf. Arnou, *Désir de Dieu*, 278.

27. Cf. 5.1 [10].6.13 for such abiding in silence.

the dawn of that light that is the One. In the preceding chapter, Plotinus says of ocular vision:

One thing is an object of vision for it, the form of the sensible object, another is that by means of which [i.e., light] it sees the form of it [the sensible object], which [medium] is also an object of sensation for it, while being other than the form [of the sensible object] and the cause for the form of being seen and is concomitantly seen both in the form and with the form (ἐν μὲν τῷ εἴδει καὶ ἐπὶ τοῦ εἴδους συνορώμενον); for this reason it [the light] does not yield a clear sensation of itself, because the eye is turned toward the illuminated object; but whenever it [i.e., the light] is nothing but itself, it sees it in an immediate intuition. (5.5 [32].7.2–8)[28]

Plotinus goes on to remark (lines 9–16) that, in the case of ocular vision, the eye cannot perceive light unless the light is present to or manifest in some material substrate. For this reason, we would not even see the sun, if the sun consisted of nothing but light.[29] If the sun were pure light, then it would be in no form appropriate to other visible things and would perhaps itself be purely visible. Other visible things would have their visibility derivatively as they are not pure light.

Plotinus pursues an analogy to ocular vision:

This then is what the seeing of Intellect is like; this sees by another light the things illuminated by that first nature [i.e., the One or Good as the sun of the intelligible universe], and sees the light in them; when it turns its attention

---

28. My translation.

29. Armstrong, trans., vol. 5, 176 note 1, takes the medium in question to be not light but another medium (such as air) and remarks: "Here Plotinus is assuming, for the purposes of his illustration, the common doctrine, that sight takes place through a medium. But in his fuller (and earlier) discussion of the problem in 4.5 (29) he rejects the medium theory and holds that sense-perception takes place through the universal sympathy of the All." It is unnecessary to see in this passage an un-Plotinian concession to a popular view. Indeed this interpretation would destroy the analogy intended in this chapter: illumined sensible object :: illumined intelligible object; light as medium of sensible vision :: light as medium of intelligible vision; pure sun :: the One (see HBT 3 b 409 *ad* 7.16). In line 20, Intellect looks toward the medium of vision (and sees the One as pure light); to preserve the analogy, the instrument of vision in line 3 must also be light, seen first as instrument of seeing and being seen and then as light *qua* light.

to the nature of the things illuminated, it sees the light less; but if it abandons the things it sees and looks at the medium by which it sees them, it looks at pure light and the source of light. (lines 16–21)[30]

Light (both sensible and intelligible) is for Plotinus initially a marginal intentional object of our awareness. It may, however, become the focal intentional object. Light is seen concomitantly with, or together with (συνορώμενον), what is originally the focal intentional object of awareness, the illumined object. Here Plotinus makes use of the verb συνορᾶν. To the Greekless reader it should be explained that the verb in question is a compound consisting of a prefix, *sun-* or "with" and a suffix, *horan*, or "see." The phrase "seen together with" is a participial form of this verb. The light is seen by the eye (line 5) both "in the form" (ἐν τῷ εἴδει) and "upon the form" (ἐπὶ τοῦ εἴδους). As long as the light is seen "in" the illuminated objects, it remains at the margin of awareness. When, however, our regard is directed to the light as "upon" these objects, the light is in the process of becoming the focal intentional object of awareness. Similarly, Intellect (lines 18–21) initially sees the light that is the Good or One as "in" the illumined objects (ἐν ἐκείνοις) but, when it directs it vision "toward" (πρὸς) the illuminated objects, it sees the light less. When it abandons these objects and attends to the light itself, it looks "into" (εἰς) the light and sees the light itself.[31]

In the first chapter, I remarked that Form as cause or instrument could be discussed in terms of explanation or use, but that Form may also be regarded as an intrinsically valuable object of intellective vision and understood under the category of enjoyment.[32] In the last chapter, in the examination of light, we discovered that, on the model of illumination and reflection, the intrinsic value of Form is built into the very structure of creation, so that its value for causation need not, as on the model of representation, be considered in abstraction from its intrinsic value. To create, it has only to be what it is in its intrinsic value.[33]

30. Trans. Armstrong (I have supplied the material in square brackets).
31. For the kind of phenomenological description that I bring to this passage, see Husserl, *Ideen*, 56–58.
32. See pp. 15–16 above.
33. See pp. 28–32; 36–39 above.

In the present chapter we shall continue our presentation of light as that symbol of the intelligible world that, more than any other, possesses for Plotinus the greatest degree of ontological adequacy. We shall show more exactly how the image of light is such a valuable vehicle for Plotinus' account. When light is merely the instrument of our being able to see, when it discharges that function of use, it hovers at the margin of awareness. When, however, it is seen in and of itself as the focal intentional object, its role as instrument, use, and cause is suspended in our enjoyment of it as an intrinsically valuable object of vision.

From 4.5 [29].7 and 5.5 [32].8 we have seen that the presence of light, which is incorporeal, cannot be understood as local presence.[34] This understanding of the presence of light accords well with the account of the perception of light that we have examined in 5.5 [32].7, and that immediately precedes the injunction to abide in silence of the eighth chapter. Thus we need not go anywhere to pursue the light. It is always there. We need not even change the direction in which we are looking. We may rather abide or remain. Indeed the light is not only there in that it illumines the landscape. It is there as an intentional object of our awareness, even if only as a non-thematic object belonging to the margin of consciousness. If, however, we address our regard to the light itself, it becomes the intentional object of focal awareness. What also emerges from 5.5 [32].7 is the character of light as that which is eminently *self-manifesting*. The object seen by means of light distracts our regard from the light until, in our abiding, we practise *openness*.[35]

The verb *sun(h)oran,* "see together with," then is used to describe the perception of light by the eye and of the One by Intellect. Another verb with the same prefix (*sun-*), *suneinai* (*einai* means "to be") is employed to describe the presence of light or of any entity that may be understood on the model of light. The light is said to "be with" that which it illumines, even as it is "seen with" the illumined objects.

In 6.4 [22].9, as we saw in the last chapter,[36] powers proceed from the intelligible world as light from light, in such a way that they are not cut off from but are rather yoked to those essences in dynamic continuity and real presence. The essences are said to "be with" the

---

34. See pp. 25–28; 45–46 above.
35. Cf. 6.7 [38].36.20–21 for the One as light itself the object of vision.
36. pp. 31–32.

powers (συνοῦσαι ταῖς δυνάμεσι, lines 27–28). The One is said to "be with" (σύνεστιν) all things, even if they are ignorant of the One.[37] Thus when Form as light is "seen with" the illumined objects, we are seeing that which "is with," is truly present to, these objects.

We have already observed the reciprocal usages of "abiding" to describe illumination and to describe a meditative practice directed at return to the source. Here we see a complementary use of two words, one perceptual or epistemological, the other ontological, both beginning with the prefix *sun-*, to describe both presence and intentionality. "Seeing with" explicates "being with."

Presence to the illumined object in the sense of *suneinai*, "being with," is a projection outward in dynamic continuity of that more radical form of "being with" that consists in the indwelling of the light in the source of light. It will be recalled that in 5.4 [7].2 Plotinus states the principle that every essence produces from its inherent activity an activity directed externally that is in dynamic continuity with that essence. As fire while it abides produces heat, so does the One in its abiding produce Intellect from the activity that is together with itself (ἐκ τῆς...συνούσης ἐνεργείας, lines 34–35). As we saw above, the One is said to "be with" all things, even if they are ignorant of the One.[38]

When our "seeing with" is directed to light, not as marginal to awareness, but as focus of consciousness, we are advancing in the direction of seeing the light not merely in its presence to other things but in its own being as it inheres in the source of light. The sense of "with" changes radically between the instance of seeing the light as it is with the illumined and as it is with its very source. Yet the one sense of withness is deeply founded in and continuous with the other.

To return to the source is also to "be with" (συνεῖναι) the source. Thus (in a passage which again offers fire and heat as an example of procession in dynamic continuity),[39] Plotinus says, of the presence of Intellect to the One and Soul to Intellect, that the begotten's love for the begetter is such that the former "is with" (σύνεστιν) the latter in such closeness that they are separated by otherness alone.[40]

Thus to "be with" (συνεῖναι) contains three moments: (1) an indwelling as of light in the source; (2) a procession from the source in

37. 6.9 [9].7.29.
38. 6.9 [9].7.29.
39. 5.1 [10].6.30–36.
40. 5.1 [10].6.50–54. cf. 1.2 [19].4.12–16 for the dependence of Soul on Intellect; the Soul's good is to "be with" (συνεῖναι) that to which it is most akin.

which the source remains present and in dynamic continuity with the product; (3) a return to the source. These senses may be distinguished but we must remember that each moment in the Plotinian trinity of abiding, procession, and return is poised in an internal relationship with the others.

These three moments of "being with" find their complements in the Plotinian vocabulary of consciousness. We have already gained some familiarity with this in our consideration of "seeing with" (συν-ορᾶν). This vocabulary is filled out by other words that also have the prefix *sun-* or "with": *sunaisthêsis* (and *sunaisthanesthai*) and *sunesis* (and *sunienai*). These words are used to describe: (1) the source's sense of being at one with itself;[41] (2) the product's awareness of the source as a marginal object of consciousness;[42] and (3) the product's unreflected awareness of its being at one with its source.[43] We shall return to this complex of vocabulary in our treatment of love in the fifth chapter.

In 5.5 [32].7.5–6 then, the light is "seen with" the illumined object. This "seeing with" (*sunoran*) is the epistemological expression of ontological "being with" (*sunousia*). "Being with" is associated with the "abiding" of the source. The light abides with the source, even in its procession. We have seen how the complex of ontological (*sunousia*) and epistemological (*sunoran, sunaisthêsis, sunesis*) vocabulary, each term of which is initiated by the prefix *-sun,* or "with," serves as an elastic inventory of presence and dependence, describing the mutual presence of source and product without confusing the one with the other.

---

41. 5.3 [49].13.16–22 where συνεῖναι and συναίσθησις are together used to describe this moment in Intellect (cf. Schroeder, *Synousia, Synaisthêsis* and *Synesis*," 685; 6.7 [38].41.17–27 for συνεῖναι, συναίσθησις and σύνεσις of Intellect (cf. Schroeder, *Synousia, Synaisthêsis* and *Synesis*," 686; cf. 5.4 [7].2.13–19 and Schroeder, "*Synousia, Synaisthêsis* and *Synesis*," 692 for a kind of συναίσθησις in the One corresponding to συνουσία as the radical coherence in the One of attributes later to be explicated in the Intellect); see Chapter 5, note 81 below.

42. Cf. 6.7 [38].16.19–22 of Intellect's awareness (συναίσθησις) of the One (cf. Schroeder, "*Synousia, Synaisthêsis* and *Synesis*," 687; 1.6 [1].2.3 of the soul's awareness (συνίημι) of Beauty (cf. Schroeder, "*Synousia, Synaisthêsis* and *Synesis*," 687; 3.5 [50].1.18, again for the soul's awareness of Beauty (cf. Schroeder, "*Synousia, Synaisthêsis* and *Synesis*," 687–88.

43. 5.8 [31].11.21–24 of the soul's unreflected awareness (συναίσθησις and σύνεσις) in union with the Form of Beauty (cf. Schroeder "*Synousia, Synaisthêsis* and *Synesis*," 688; and 6.9 [9].3.49 – 6.9 [9].4.3 for unreflected awareness (σύνεσις) in union with the One.

Plato uses the term *parousia* ("presence") asymmetrically, as describing the relation of the Form to the particular[44] but not the presence of the particular to the Form. Plotinus, when he uses the noun *parousia* or the verb *pareinai* ("to be present"), often carefully qualifies the word to strip it of spatial associations. Again, he wishes to avoid confusion of immaterial Form with the material particulars. Plotinus says of the presence of the One: "It is really a wonder how he is present (πάρεστι) without having come, and how, though he is nowhere, there is nowhere where he is not" (5.5 [32].8.23–24). In 4.5 [29].7.42, the account of the physics of light, Plotinus is wary of using the word even of the incorporeal source of light. Yet he must have come to feel that he had sufficiently neutralised the spatial associations of the word to allow him the same elastic use that he makes of *sunousia*. Thus *parousia* may describe both the presence of the intelligible to the sensible world[45] and the presence of the sensible to the intelligible world.[46] The vocabulary of abiding and silence exhibits a similar elasticity. Even as the One (in other texts) creates in abiding and silence, so (5.5 [32].8) may we, in abiding and silence, return to the One. This vocabulary describes both the creative presence of the One to us and our contemplative presence to the One.

In the *Phaedrus*, the *Symposium*, and the *Republic*, Plato describes, in spatial imagery, the ascent of the soul to the intelligible world. Plato locates the Forms, in the *Phaedrus*, in a "place above the heavens"[47] and, in the *Republic*, in an "intelligible place."[48] Perhaps we see in Plotinus a certain resistance to the language of ascent and spatial location in Plato. If we construe the language of "abiding," "silence," "light," and the vocabulary of "being with" conspectively, we may see that, where Plato challenges us to scale daunting heights, the Plotinian universe presents a texture of penetrable depth accessible by an act of abiding in silence and thus allows us gently to return to the condition of our source.[49]

44. Cf. *Phaedo* 100d5.
45. 6.5 [23].12.1–3.
46. 6.5 [23].3.13–15.
47. 247c3; cf. 247a8–b1.
48. 508c1; 517b5.
49. Sinnige, "Metaphysical and Personal Religion," compares the circle and centre imagery in 6.9 [8].8–10 and the progress of the soul in Plato *Phaedrus* 246d6–248e3 to demonstrate this contrast between height and inwardness. Sinnige also compares 1.7 [54].1.21–28, where the centre and circle imagery is combined with the figure of sun and light, with *Republic* 507a1–509b10 where (152) "the sun is in his [Plato's] simile not a centre of emanation for hypostases of being."

The notion of abiding in luminous silence preserves the sovereignty and intrinsic value of Form in creation. Abiding in silence is also the avenue of our return, as we open ourselves to the enjoyment of Form as of intrinsic value, apart from its uses in explanation.

We have seen how the language of light is a crucial component of that larger complex of vocabulary that includes abiding and silence. We also know that reflection, as an instance of light, is another vital component of this semantic field. We have yet to examine the nexus between reflection and silence. Now reflection may be either an ontological or an epistemological term. A mirror may reflect. So may a mind. If a surface is to reflect, it must be smooth, undisturbed, calm, and silent. This quietness may belong to mental as well as to any other kind of reflection.

Plotinus asks whether a good man, that he may be good, must be aware of his goodness (1.4 [46].9–10). Now a man may be healthy without being aware of his health. If a man is healthy, however, he is healthy whether he sleeps or is awake. Yet surely wisdom must be active and therefore belong to a conscious and active state. Therefore a man asleep would not be wise. Yet wisdom belongs to the very substance of man's intellective phase. It is therefore always actively engaged by the higher soul, even if the lower soul is not conscious of it.

Awareness of the noetic activity of the higher soul may arise in the lower soul when the latter reflects that activity as in a mirror. It may be so reflected when the reflective surface is in a state of quiet (ἡσυχα-ζον), i.e., is not disturbed.[50] So the part of the soul that reflects this higher activity must observe quiet or silence (ἡσυχίαν – ἄγοντος, 1.4. [46].10.13). Only then may the mind-picture or image of this higher activity appear. If, however, this mirror is broken, let us say because the harmony of the body is disturbed, then the image no longer is visible.

Yet, whether the image appears or not, the activity that is its source continues. This superior noetic activity is the wisdom and hence the goodness of the good man. Therefore the man is good, whether he is aware of his goodness (i.e., whether his lower soul reflects this) or not. The source of the reflection is there, as is its ability to illumine the mirror with its reflection, whether there is a reflective surface or not. We have seen in the second chapter that for Plotinus illumination

50. 1.4 [46].10.10.

is an effect of the source alone, not a joint effect proceeding from the luminous source in concert with the illumined objects.[51] This is why the example of the mirror is especially valuable for the completion of Plotinus' argument. The goodness of the good man (his superior noetic activity) is as independent from its manifestation in ordinary waking consciousness as is the source of light and reflection from its manifestation in a reflective surface.

However, the mirror need not serve merely as an example or simile. The Greek words κάτοπτρον and ἔσοπτρον need not refer to the mirror as artifact, but may signify any reflective surface (e.g., water).[52] The illumination and reflection of this passage indeed satisfy the preconditions for illumination. Clearly, as we are concerned with soul and mind, the light in question cannot be corporeal. (Nor is it merely a matter of abstract mental processes, as Plotinus stresses the unity of being and thought at the noetic level.)[53] It may also be seen as uniquely the effect of the source. So we need not read 1.4 [46].10 as saying that the soul is only metaphorically a mirror. In so far as it satisfies the conditions of reflection as an imaging in the real presence of colour and light it really is a mirror. Here again we may see how (considering reflection as an instance of illumination) the language of light allows Plotinus to be a realist.[54]

We have seen above that Plotinus distinguishes between the reflected image as a natural image and the artistic artifact as an artificial image.[55] Plato, in a famous passage in the *Republic*, argues that a painting of a bed represents a third degree from reality: the Form of bed is first, the artificial bed, as imitation of the first, stands second

51. pp. 27–28.

52. Ovid *Met.* III.344–48; Pausanias ix.31.7 for water as such a surface; cf. Aristophanes *Acharnians* 1128–29 for a shield as a reflective surface in divination. The word ἔσοπτρον may refer equally either to the mirror as artifact or to water as a reflective surface, *vide* Plutarch *Quaest. Conviv.* 682e11–12. See Schroeder, "Representation and Reflection," 55.

53. 1.4 [46].10.5–6.

54. Cf. 4.3 [27].30 for a further example of intellectual reflection: the "discursive sequel (λόγος) to an act of inuitive thought is received into the imaginative faculty ... The *logos* deploys the thought and shows it to the imaginative faculty as though in a mirror" (Blumenthal, *Plotinus' Psychology*, 88). Perhaps in 1.4 [46].10, as in 4.3 [27].30, one of the causes of the disruption of reflection is the arrival of sensation, cf. Blumenthal *Plotinus' Psychology*, 89).

55. Cf. 5.8 [31].12.15–20 and p. 42 above.

and the painting of the bed, as imitation of the second, stands third.[56]
Plato extends this line of thinking to art generally.[57]

Plotinus must see the sentiment of this passage as at variance with
the essential tendency of Plato's thought. How could the philosopher
who most understood Form see art as mere representation? Plotinus
asserts his dependence upon the authority of Plato but with the re-
servation that Plato is not always quite as explicit as he would like him
to be.[58] Plotinus' discussion of artistic imitation intends not a departure from that authority, but a deeper understanding of Plato's intention. Thus the musician who knows that the unheard sounds of
the intelligible world are sweeter will for that reason be stirred when
he attends to sensible melodies. Two persons may look at the same
portrait and yet one will know rapture, while the other is unmoved.
The first is like the musician, for he experienced recollection (*anamnêsis*) of his beloved who was portrayed in the painting.[59]

Plotinus must here be thinking of the *anamnêsis* that Cebes has
of Simmias when he sees his portrait in *Phaedo* 73e9–10. Of course, in
the *Phaedo* the intention is to demonstrate the *anamnêsis* of Form. As
we saw in the first chapter, Platonic *anamnêsis* is understood by Plotinus, not as referring to an antenatal act of cognition but to the
engagement of a superior awareness on the part of the higher soul
which is always contemplating intelligible reality.[60] Plotinus asserts
that the great sculptor Pheidias, when he produced his statue of Zeus,
did not look toward any model in the world of sense, but rather
portrayed Zeus as he would seem if he chose to appear among us.[61]
In this case, the artist creates, in his statue, the vehicle of Plotinian
anamnêsis.

We should recall, however, that Plotinus distinguishes between what
we have been calling representation and reflection. On Plotinus' view,
the painting of the bed in the *Republic* may indeed be at a third degree
of reality in so far as it is merely representational. By appeal to this
distinction, Plotinus might remain faithful to Plato and accept his

56. 597b2–e5.
57. *Republic* 592e6 ff.
58. 5.1 [10].8.10–14; cf. the ironic statement (4.8 [6].1.23–26) that Plato said many
fine things about the soul so that we may hope to gain something clear from him upon
this subject!
59. 2.9 [33].16.39–56.
60. pp. 11–12 above.
61. 5.8 [31].1.38–40.

master's interpretation of the painting of the bed. What he implicitly does not accept is the extension of this model to all of art.[62]

We are now in a position to approach a fruitful paradox in the thought of Plotinus. We have so far distinguished between two models of imitation in Plotinus: representation and reflection. Representation belongs to art or craft (τέχνη), and reflection to nature (φύσις). While in reflection the attributes of the subject are truly present in the image in dynamic continuity, representation introduces a gulf between the original and the image, reducing the attributes to a divided plurality of analytic concepts.

However, if art can transcend representation, could it not produce an artifact that would, like nature, not merely represent, but reflect intelligible reality? Plotinus indeed offers us this interpretation of art as reflection:

And I think that the wise men of old, who made temples and statues in the wish that gods should be present to them, looking to the nature of the All, had in mind that the nature of soul is everywhere easy to attract, but that if someone were to construct something sympathetic to it and able to receive a part of it, it would of all things receive soul most easily. That which is sympathetic to it is what imitates it in some way, like a mirror able to catch [the reflection] of a form. Yes, the nature of the All, too, made all things skillfully in imitation of the [intelligible] realities of which it had the rational principles, and when each thing in this way had become a rational principle in matter, shaped according to that which was before matter, it linked it with that god in conformity with whom it came into being and to whom the soul looked and whom it had in its making. (4.3 [27].11.1–12)

Reflection differs from representation in virtue of its direct relation between original and image. Yet a mirror allows me to see things indirectly. Merely representational art differs from reflection because the realization of the image requires mediation on the part of the artist. Such a work of representational art also allows me to see something indirectly.

62. For a fuller discussion of these aspects of Plotinus on artistic imitation, see Rich, "Plotinus and the Theory of artistic imitation"; Plotinus, like Plato, despises art that represents sensible models, cf. 4.3 [27].10.17–19; 4.3 [27].18.1–8; for further examples of the higher human art, derived from intuition of intelligible form, cf. 5.8 [31].1.32–40: cf. Fazzo, *La giustificazione delle imagine*, 151–80.

The image, whether in representation or in reflection, can allow me an indirect view of sensible objects. The very absence of a human artist prepares us to see in nature the direct relationship between original and image that we know from the model of reflection as existing between an immaterial entity like Beauty and its instantiation in nature. Yet in art transcending mere representation, the relation between transcendent beauty and its artistic image is also direct and transcendent beauty is reflected in the work of art. If transcendent beauty is not merely represented but reflected in nature and in art, then it must be truly present both to the mirror of art and the mirror of nature.

Such reflection, whether in nature or in art, requires not one but two reflective surfaces: the mirror of art or nature and the mirror of the beholder's mind. We may see a sensible object indirectly by means of a mirror. In the case of an immaterial entity, two mirrors may reflect it directly: the natural object or the work of art and the human mind. The presence of transcendent beauty to the beautiful object calms and opens our minds so that they directly reflect that beauty. Indeed we have seen from 1.4 [46].10 that the mind may really be a mirror as it practises quiet or silence.[63]

In the *Phaedo*, the first act of *anamnêsis* is to recollect the beloved from seeing his cloak or his lyre. We have here a simple act of association. A second act of *anamnêsis* is prompted by his seeing a likeness of Cebes.[64] Now a purely representational likeness or photograph might succeed in inducing recollection of the type we encounter in the first case. Yet we would surely wish that the vehicle of *anamnêsis* would be more than a simple act of association. The artist, for example, can produce a merely external likeness of his subject. By the use of such devices as expression, however, he can represent deeper qualities. In this case the artist is looking to that invisible subject of

---

63. In 1.4 [46].10, self-conscious awareness is seen to impede activity, e.g., the reader's awareness that he is reading, the brave man's awareness of his courage, is seen to impede activity. As the mirroring of higher noetic activity is an awareness of this activity, it might be objected that this awareness would be, not a means of anagogical ascent, but of detraction from superior awareness. This objection fails if we keep the context in mind: such awareness on the part of the higher soul would have this effect but the lower soul would surely be exalted by it. Plotinus is making the point that awareness of its activity on the part of the higher soul would be distracting to the higher soul.

64. 72e3–73e4.

which both his painting and the physical presence of the subject in the sensible world are mirror images.

In a sense, even the human subject as present in nature mirrors his unseen parts in greater or lesser degrees. For this reason a face is, by virtue of its expression, sometimes beautiful and sometimes not.[65]

It must by now be obvious that, when we are speaking of representation and reflection, we are speaking of two *models* of imitation. We must not confuse these models with particular examples. Thus a work of art may (if it fulfils the conditions of reflection and illumination) serve as a mirror, or a mirror image may (if regarded as if disconnected from its source) be viewed as if it were a work of representational art. Earlier it was remarked that the route to the proper understanding of the distinction between representation and reflection was through epistemological rather than ontological considerations. However, the ontological aspect is also crucial. Epistemology and ontology, knowing and being, achieve a splendid coincidence in the Plotinian theory of imitation.

The structure of reflection is, as we have said, triadic, consisting of subject of reflection, mind as mirror, and nature or art as mirror. Even at this point we are not to forget that mind *is* a mirror, i.e., it is not just *metaphorically* a mirror. Think of a triangle. At its base, we have at one end the mirror of mind and at the other the mirror of nature (or of art fulfilling the conditions of nature). Now draw a line at some point above but parallel to the base line connecting the two sides of the triangle. Now the distance between the two ends of this line is shorter than the two ends of the base. If we were to continue adding such lines above this point, each line would be shorter than the last. Eventually there is, at the peak of the triangle, a coincidence. Mind as mirror and nature as mirror meet at this omega point of illumination.

In the case of representation, the artist intervenes between the subject and the image, analysing attributes that inhere as a unity in the original into a plurality of discrete attributes of imitation, blue into daub of blue paint, curly into wavy lines, and so on. In the case of reflection, the attributes of the image are truly present in the image so that, for example, the blue in the subject's eyes is truly present in

65. 1.6 [1].1.37–40.

the image and stands in a relation of dynamic continuity with it. Both images divide the original into attributes of imitation that in their aggregate constitute an image in quasi-unity. Surely it is the image as a whole and not its constituent parts which serves an anagogical function? Thus in the case of the image in reflection, even though its various attributes exhibit one by one the real presence of an attribute in the subject of imitation, taken one by one they could not lead the soul to their source.

Now, the lines we have drawn across the triangle are arbitrary. We may think of the ascent as exhibiting the same dynamic continuity that was displayed in the creation, the procession of the image in reflection. If we think of the various attributes of the image as a refraction in multiplicity of what inheres in unity in the original, then we must see that at each degree of ascent these become re-unified by degrees and point anagogically to a unity above themselves. Thus as the ontic and epistemic mirrors move toward coincidence, so does the mimetic composition of reflection move progressively toward that same point.

It would be a mistake to think of mirroring or reflection as belonging only to the structure of imitation. In the subject itself, where all is held in a unity of mutual implication and all relationships are internal, each attribute or aspect mirrors all the others. What is more, since it mirrors, not only all the others, but the all, it must also mirror itself. Thus in Intellect the Forms (which are also intellects)

See all things, not those to which coming to be, but those to which real being belongs, and they see themselves in other things; or all things there are transparent, and there is nothing dark or opaque; everything and all things are clear to the inmost part to everything; for light is transparent to light. Each there has everything in itself and sees all things in every other, so that all are everywhere and each and every one is all and the glory is unbounded. A different kind of being stands out in each, but in each all are manifest (ἐμφαίνει). (5.8 [31].4.3–11)

The verb here translated "are manifest" (ἐμφαίνειν) is used of appearance in reflective surfaces.[66] Plotinus continues: "Here, however,

---

66. Plato *Republic* 402b6; Plotinus 1.4 [46].10.14.

one part would not come from another, and each would be only a part; but there each comes only from the whole and is part and whole at once: it has the appearance of a part, but the whole is seen in it (ἐνορᾶται) by a penetrating look" (lines 21–24). The verb here rendered as "is seen in" (ἐνορᾶσθαι) is also used of appearing in mirrors.[67] Plotinus also says: "All things of this kind there are like images seen by their own light (οἷον ἀγάλματα παρ'αὐτῶν ἐνορώμενα)" (lines 42–44). Again the verb ἐνορᾶσθαι, which belongs to reflection, is used. Notice the boldness here of saying that the Forms, in so far as they image each other in reflection, are said to be images. How strange this must seem to us who are so used to the idea that the Form must be original while the particular is image! Here the Form is both.

Let us consider the significance of this internal mirroring or reflection in Intellect. The interior reflection in Intellect is the ground of all mirroring in our minds or in art or nature. We have also seen that it is the internal "abiding" of the light in the source which is the ground of our "abiding"; its "silence" the ground of our "silence" and our return. Moreover, the "being with" or "withness" (*sunousia*) internal to the source is the ground of our "being with" the source and our "seeing" the light "together with" (*sunoran*) the illumined objects. We are tempted to see abiding from the horizon of procession, and reflection from the horizon of the created image. Yet these are grounded in the same character for each is inherent in the source itself. In this inherence, however, the character of the source *qua* source is bracketed so that we may consider it in its sovereign value, independent of any of its uses in explanation. When thus regarded in its intrinsic value, we see it as not merely an instrument, but the final goal of enjoyment.

Plotinus' whole concern not to confuse Form with the particular, immaterial with material, and original with the image has set us up to expect his universe to exhibit asymmetry. The predicate "X" will be used in one sense of the source and in another of the product. So, in "emanationist" imagery expressing the procession of sensible from intelligible reality, the stream may proceed from the spring, but from a spring that is immaterial, not a material spring of the kind we find in this world. Yet the language of light, including reflection, enjoys a privileged position in the hierarchy of figurative language. For light

67. 4.5 [29].7.45; 1.4 [46].10.15.

truly *is* immaterial; it truly *does* abide while an act directed externally is projected from it, etc. Moreover, contrary to our expectation, the language that lies at the heart of illumination, abiding, silence, light from light, and reflection allows of a symmetry of predication. The vital freight of this symmetry is that, instead of looking at Form from the horizon of the particular, we may both guard its intrinsic value and yet make meaningful statements about the Form as it is in its own nature and apart from its relationship to the particular to which it stands in an asymmetrical relation of imitation.

In our previous discussion of 5.5 [32].8 and the prescription to abide in silence if we would know the One, it was suggested that this imagery offered a more gentle approach than that which might otherwise be afforded by Platonic philosophy. In the place of challenging heights, we were offered accessible depths. Even the notions of depth and inwardness, being spatial metaphors, may be rather inappropriate. The imagery of light, abiding, and silence is precisely designed to obviate suggestion of place in the presence of Form. Light is incorporeal and is present not in place but by virtue of its activity, abiding in continuity with its source.

Plotinus speculates: "If it was possible for Intellect to abide in that nowhere – I do not mean that Intellect is in place: it is no more in place than he [the One] is – it would always behold him, or rather not behold him, but be one with him, not two" (5.5 [32].8.18–22).

To be nowhere, to have no place on which to stand, is disorienting and occasions the failure of union with the One. Of the soul's quest for the One, Plotinus says:

What then could the One be, and what nature could it have? There is nothing surprising in its being difficult to say, when it is not even easy to say what Being or Form is; but we do have a knowledge based upon the Forms. But in proportion as the soul goes towards the formless, since it is utterly unable to comprehend it because it is not delimited and, so to speak, stamped by a richly varied stamp, it slides away and is afraid that it may have nothing at all. (6.9 [9].3.1–6)

And so it seeks the solidity and definition of the sensible world.

Plotinus interprets (6.9 [9].11) the oath of silence proper to the mysteries to mean that we must not trivialise the experience of the One which rests upon a union transcending seeing and being seen, beyond awareness and desire, beyond all limits "in the silent desert" (ἡσυχῇ ἐν ἐρήμῳ).[68] The desert offers a splendid image of what Plotinus wishes to convey: total absence of things, the daring embrace of formlessness, the address to Form not as that which informs but as the source of our transformation. This silence is not merely the absence of demiurgic busyness; it is the silence and abiding that precedes all creation.[69]

We may ask whether there is a tension between the apparently gentle prescription of silence and the unsettling encounter with the Form as formless. The practice of silence is, as we have seen, an act of openness, of allowing light or form to reveal itself. Yet a corollary of that very openness is that we not impose form upon the formless, that we encounter the formlessness of form through an opening of our horizon and emptiness of determination. In 6.9 [9].9–11, Plotinus argues that when we seek to behold the One or Good as an object we must fail in our quest. It is in entering into ourselves that we, in converse with the One, become "beyond essence" (ἐπέκεινα τῆς οὐσίας, 6.9 [9].11.42). This is to say that the human soul, in union with the One or Good, admits the same description as the Good of Plato's *Republic*.[70] We may think of Heidegger's observation that Plato's phrase well describes the transcendence of determination on the part of *Dasein*.[71] The encounter with the Good, not as a defined thing but as formless, is also an encounter with ourselves. We are not things. In our fear of the abyss of indeterminacy, we may seek solid ground in the world of things. When we do so, we are also seeking to reify ourselves, to escape authenticity.

We shall see in the next chapter that the encounter with formlessness and thus with ourselves has much to do with the origin of

---

68. 6.9 [9].11.13.

69. For the One as the formless (ἀνείδεον, ἄμορφον) principle that confers Form, cf. further 6.7 [38].17.18; 17.36; 28.28; 32.9; 33.37 and Hadot, "Structure et Thèmes," 658. Form in Greek thought is generally associated with limit, so that it may be seen as itself limited. Plotinus asks whether that which limits must itself be limited. He reasons that since Intellect is form and essence generated from the One, the One as source of these is neither (it is ἀνείδεον). As Intellect is limited or finite (ὡρισμένον), the One is not limited or finite (5.5 [32].6.1–7). Thus the formlessness of the One is associated with its infinity. We should doubtless now accept the view that the One is infinite, not by extrinsic, but by intrinsic denomination; for bibliography on this question, see Blumenthal, "Plotinus in the Light of Scholarship," 551.

70. 509b9.

71. Heidegger, *Grundprobleme*, 436.

philosophical language. If I fall away from what is beyond essence and determination, I shall ask myself, "What have I seen?" I shall seek in words that element of definition and determinacy the lack of which caused me to fall from the vision of the Good.

The address to Form requires us to understand that, taken in itself, or from its own horizon, Form is not cause. Thus: "For to say that it is the cause is not to predicate something incidental of it but of us, because we have something from it while that One is in itself" (6.9 [9].3.49–51). Indeed, as we have seen from 6.9 [9].3.1–6, Form is not for itself form, but only for us. Thus also the One is not an intelligible object in itself, but only for another (νοητὸν ἑτέρῳ)[72] *viz.* Intellect.

We have seen that the human soul may return to the One, her creator, in entering upon that silence and abiding that precedes the creation and must, if it is to be enjoyed, be seen without reference to the creation. Yet it is precisely in entering upon this silence, in which all thought of the creation must be suspended that, in grand paradox, the soul joins the One in an act of creation that proceeds as a consequence of the very being of the One. So it is that the soul, pregnant in her contact with the One, begets gods in silence, begets beauty, begets justice, begets virtue.[73]

Indeed each soul may reflect, in her fallen condition, that it was she who "made all living things herself, breathing life into them, those that the earth feeds and those that are nourished by the seas and the divine stars in the sky; she made the sun herself, and this great heaven, and adorned it herself" (5.1 [10].2.1–5).[74] Yet while the thought of her role in the creation may serve the anagogic purpose of leading the soul to her source, the ascent is accomplished only by quiet or silence (ἡσυχία) and illumination:

Let not only its encompassing body and the body's raging sea be quiet, but all its environment: the earth quiet, and the sea and air quiet, and the heaven itself at peace. Into this heaven at rest let it imagine soul as if flowing in from outside, pouring in and entering it everywhere and illuminating it: as the rays of the sun light up a dark cloud, and make it shine and give it a golden look, so soul entering into the body of heaven gives it life and gives it immortality and wakes what lies inert. (5.1 [10].2.14–23)

72. 5.6 [1].2.10.
73. 6.9 [9].9.18–19.
74. Trans. Armstrong slightly modified.

And so it is that, far from the busy ministrations of the Demiurge, Plotinus marries felicitously the moments of creation and contemplation, preserving the integrity and purity of each. If, reflects Plotinus, we were to ask Nature why she creates, she would reply:

"You ought not to ask, but to understand in silence, you, too, just as I am silent (σιωπῶ) and not in the habit of talking. Understand what, then? That what comes into being is what I see in my silence (σιωπώσης), an object of contemplation which comes to be naturally, and that I, originating from this sort of contemplation have a contemplative nature. And my act of contemplation makes what it contemplates, as the geometers draw their figures while they contemplate. But I do not draw, but as I contemplate, the lines which bound bodies come to be as if they fell from my contemplation. What happens to me is what happens to my mother and the beings that generated me, for they, too, derive from contemplation, and it is no action of theirs which brings about my birth; they are greater rational principles, and as they contemplate themselves I come to be." (3.8 [30].4.3–14)

Nature, begotten, not made, proceeds from contemplation in silence and herself gives birth from silent contemplation. Light from light, begotten, not made, when we abide in that silence we in transformation join in the creation of the world.

IV

Word

PORPHYRY TELLS US[1] HOW, when he was perplexed concerning the relation between soul and body, Plotinus continued to answer his questions for three days, much to the annoyance of one Thaumasius, who preferred a set lecture. The Socratic spirit cannot have been much absent from the circle of Plotinus and we can often trace the apparent give and take of discussion in the *Enneads*.[2]

1. *Vita Plotini* 13.

2. See Hadot, "Philosophie, Dialectique, Rhétorique," 152–53 on this passage as an illustration of dialectical method (*zêtêma*) in Plotinus. Plotinus interpreted the text at hand in an interlocutory manner and encouraged his students to engage in original enquiry (ζητεῖν), so that his seminar was often disrupted (Porphyry, *Vita Plotini* 3.35–38; Goulet-Cazé *"Vie de Plotin,"* 250–51 on the collective character of the work in Plotinus' circle). Plotinus based his writings on discussions in his seminar, cf. Porphyry, *Vita Plotini* 5, 13, 14. If we use the word "school" to describe the group about Plotinus, we should be careful to understand that it was neither a preparation for young persons wishing to become professional philosophers, nor led by the holder of a municipal or imperial chair of philosophy, cf. Goulet-Cazé, *"Vie de Plotin,"* 231–57. Bréhier, *Philosophie de Plotin,* 13, remarks, "la philosophie de Plotin est comme presque toutes les philosophies de l'antiquité, d'abord une philosophie parlée." Cilento, "Stile, Linguaggio, Poesia," 201–2 remarks dogmatically that the apparent reflections of philosophical conversation in Plotinus may be merely an expository device resembling the diatribes of the Cynics and Stoics; they are, in any case, difficult to identify, cf. Cilento, "Stile e linguaggio nella filosofia di Plotino," 29. For examples of how discussion in the Plotinian circle may be reflected in the *Enneads*, see 4.3 [27].1.17 and Helleman-Elgersma, *Soul-Sisters*, 190; 5.1 [10].7 and Schroeder, "Conversion and Consciousness;" 6.7 [38].24.18; 6.8 [39].7.16; 6.7 [38].29.11–12 and Hadot, "Structure et Thèmes," 645–46. Hadot, *Exercices Spirituels,* insists that, when reading ancient philosophy, we locate it within the oral tradition and practice of the ancient school, the end of which is not merely the communication of a body of doctrine, but the spiritual transformation of the pupil. He remarks: "Au fond, bien que tout écrit soit un monologue, l'oeuvre philosophique

Yet if silence is the beginning and the end of Plotinian philosophizing, we may well ask, why are Plotinus and his circle in Rome so
very loquacious? What can be the status of the word or of speech in
Plotinus' thinking? Further, for Plotinus, the One, the ultimate subject
of his discourse, is finally ineffable. Why not then take refuge in
mystical silence?[3]

In treating of the One, Plotinus asks: "How then do we speak about
it? Indeed we say something about it (τι περὶ αὐτοῦ), but we do not
say the One itself (οὐ μὴν αὐτὸ λέγομεν), nor do we have knowledge
or thought of the One itself" (5.3 [49].14.1–3).[4]

In this passage Plotinus distinguishes two forms of speech concerning the One: (1) to speak about the One, or discuss the One (*legein
peri* and the genitive); (2) to say the One, or disclose the One (*legein*
and the accusative). He allows that we may discuss the One, but not
in such a way that we may disclose it (6.7 [38].38.4–5): "We predicate
the good concerning it without saying itself" (Λέγομεν δὲ τἀγαθὸν
περὶ αὐτοῦ λέγοντες οὐκ αὐτό). Harder construes:[5] Λέγομεν τἀγαθὸν
περὶ Αὐτοῦ, i.e. Λέγομεν. Αὐτό ἐστι τὸ ἀγαθόν ("We say or predicate
the good of it, i.e., we say, it is the Good"). Thus *legein peri* ("discuss")
means to make a statement about, using the (in this case) inadmissible
copula. It is not so much that Plotinus distinguishes between *legein
peri* ("discuss") and *legein* ("disclose") as two modes of discourse about
the One. Rather, he argues that, in this instance, *legein* must always
be the equivalent of *legein peri* which involves the copula and is therefore unacceptable. Therefore the attempt at disclosure will always be
resolved in mere discussion.

Are the two uses of *legein* – "discuss" and "disclose" – ever compatible
in such a way that the distinction between them is preserved? Indeed
they are. In 3.7 [45].6.17–19 Plotinus, speaking of Intellect, says that
the statement "ἔστιν" ("it is") is most true of the things that we may

---

est toujours implicitement un dialogue," (*Exercices Spirituels*, 66). It is because of this
situational aspect that the philosophy of Plotinus and other ancient thinkers does not
present a "system" in the modern sense.

3. A large part of the present chapter is derived from Schroeder, "Saying and
Having."

4. My translation; cf. Plato *Timaeus* 28c3–5 where it is denied that it is possible to
disclose (λέγειν and the accusative) the father of the universe to all mankind; for other
references to the distrust of speech (and writing) in Plato see *Parmenides* 142a3–8 and
Letter VII, 341c4–344d2 (which Plotinus takes to be genuine).

5. HBT 3 b 514.

say about it (τῶν περὶ αὐτό) and indeed is itself (καὶ αὐτό).[6] The rigours of Eleatic logic preclude that both senses should ever be applicable to the One.

We have so far concentrated upon the differences between "discuss" and "disclose." We have seen that Plotinus concludes the first sentence of this chapter (5.3 [49].14) by saying "nor do we *have* knowledge or thought of [the One] itself." He proceeds to exhaust the possibilities of saying and having: (1) We may have the One in such a way that we may discuss it, but not disclose it. "Indeed, if we do not have (ἔχομεν) it in knowledge, do we not have it at all? But we have it thus that we may speak about [discuss] it, but not say [disclose] it. Indeed we say what it is not, but we do not say [disclose] it, so that we may speak about [discuss] it from what follows upon it. But we are not prevented from having it, even if we do not say [disclose] it" (lines 4–8).[7] Plotinus doubtless means that we may engage in discursive thought and speech concerning the One without achieving a disclosure of its true nature (as is possible in the case of Intellect). The "having" that he will allow refers to that relationship which we have to the One in the act of discussing it at all. The central question must be, why do we continue to discuss the One if our discussion may never disclose it? Is this not a fruitless and idle enterprise?[8] (2) Plotinus then introduces a fresh distinction. We may speak while being disposed toward, literally while we "have toward" (ἔχειν πρὸς) the One:[9]

But as those who become inspired and possessed (ἐνθουσιῶντες καὶ κάτοχοι) may know this much, that they have something greater [than themselves]

---

6. In this instance the sense of λέγειν περί as "discuss" is expressed with the accusative rather than with the genitive case, as in 5.3 [49].14.1–2, but the effect is the same. Sleeman and Pollet, col. 833 give "about, concerning" for περί and the genitive, and "in regard to" for περί with the accusative; see also the article under λέγειν for λέγειν περί with the accusative, col. 594.

7. My translation.

8. Language is a mode of difference and the One is itself different from all that which is derived from it. Therefore language cannot, either by means of negation or in metaphor, adequately describe the One. Yet since these are the highest capabilities of language, we should not assess them from the perspective of adequacy to the subject that they describe. Rather we should realize that the assertion that the One may not be expressed in language is, so far as the capabilities of language allow, an adequate assertion of its absolute difference as accessible to language as itself a mode of difference; cf. Beierwaltes, *Denken des Einen*, 102.

9. My translation.

within them, even if they do not know what, but from what they are moved and what they say derive a sensation of that which moves them while they are different from that, thus we are apt to be disposed toward ["have toward", ἔχειν πρὸς] it [i.e. the One], when we have pure intellect, divining that this is the inner mind, which bestows essence and the other things that are of that rank, itself not being such, as it is not these, but something greater than that which is called "being," but fuller and greater than what-is-said, because it is itself greater than speech and mind and sensation, bestowing these, while not itself being these. (lines 8–19)

Pure intellect (νοῦς καθαρός) and the inner mind (ὁ ἔνδον νοῦς) refer to a phase or power of Intellect that transcends its own nature, a sort of ambassador of the One within the structure of Intellect. Thus in 6.9 [9].3.26–27 we behold the One with pure intellect (καθαρῷ τῷ νῷ) and with the first principle of intellect (τοῦ νοῦ τῷ πρώτῳ).[10] Of course, the human soul may coincide with this phase in its ascent toward the One. It is to be observed that all the predicates here attributed to pure intellect may also be assigned to the One itself with which pure intellect, as transcendent phase or power of intellect, is in union. Thus the One is greater than being, than what-is-said and than speech, mind, and sensation. The One ultimately bestows all of these, while being none of them.

The One then (observing the equation we have just undertaken), while it is greater than being, than what-is-said, and than speech *(logos)*, thought, and sensation, bestows these (παρασχὼν ταῦτα). Thus the One gives us speech. This offers a partial answer to the question why we should undertake to discuss the One if we already know that we may not disclose it. The very fact that language belongs to the creation and is the gift of the One to us carries with it the mandate and even the imperative of theological discourse. Language, especially theological language, is not altogether our own project.

What are we to make of the fact that Plotinus says that we may speak of the One in inspiration? Armstrong[11] remarks:

This passage seems to owe something to Plato's description of the inspiration of poets in *Ion* 533–4 (cp. especially ἔνθεοι ὄντες καὶ κατεχόμενοι 533E6–7). It is interesting that Plotinus finds this poetic possession (for Plato a state far

10. Cf. 5.5 [32].8.22–23; 6.7 [38].35.19–23; and Rist, "Mysticism and Transcendence."

11. Armstrong trans., vol. 5, 120 note 3.

inferior to the clear knowledge of the philosopher) a suitable analogy for our highest awareness, that of the One, and that it is for him a kind of knowledge (though not knowledge of the One) which it certainly is not for Plato.

Is Plotinus in this passage praising poetry at the expense of philosophy? If he is, then he is advancing poetry as a way of truth at the very moment at which he has despaired of philosophy as a means of disclosing the One. A passage in Plato's *Apology*, which Plotinus may also have in mind here, describes poets as inspired (ἐνθουσιάζοντες) and, like the *Ion*, has them not understanding the meaning of what they say.[12] Both the *Ion* and the *Apology* associate poetic inspiration with prophecy.[13]

Poetry and prophecy then compete with philosophy in this passage. Who are the "we" (ἡμεῖς, line 13) who are the subject of the analogy which Plotinus is drawing? Not poets (or prophets), for that is the other term of the analogy: "we" are *like* poets, i.e., it is not the case that we *are* poets. The reference to poetic or prophetic possession in the *Ion* or the *Apology* need not mean that Plotinus is inviting us to construe "we" here as "we poets or prophets." He may simply borrow from Plato a term of the comparison. Poets and prophets lack science and knowledge. They do not know what they are saying. The comparison extends to our speaking without true knowledge. The "we" of this passage is not necessarily co-extensive with the vocation of poetry or prophecy. Plotinus is not making an abrupt transition to the truth of poetry or to a preference for poetry over philosophy. Plotinus and his circle have been discussing how we may speak of the One. It has been asserted that discussion does not disclose the One. The "we" in question is ourselves as philosophers, i.e., those who (while yet lacking science or knowledge) continue to speak because we are committed to discussing the One.

Plotinus here offers us a middle ground between discussing and disclosing the One. Philosophical language may, on the analogy of mantic inspiration, declare the One. We have thus three forms of discourse about the One: disclosure, discussion, and declaration. While disclosure may be impossible, we may yet discuss or declare.[14]

12. Cf. *Apology* 22b8 and *Ion* 534c7-d4.

13. Cf. *Ion* 534b7; 534d1 and *Apology* 22c1-2.

14. Hadot, *Exercices Spirituels*, 189 and note 18; 192 sees in this passage the possibility of speaking of (*en parler*) the One, even if we cannot say it (*le dire*). He sees our having, however, as consisting only in mystical ecstasy and does not distinguish having in the sense of that relationship to the One which is already given in philosophical discussion.

Language shares important attributes with light. Light evanesces in the act of illumination. We see, not light, but the thing illumined. Language is an instrument that illumines its objects in the same way. It is not itself a theme of awareness; it lies at the margin of consciousness.

In poetry language is thematized. Its referential purpose is devoured by its revealed transparency. The words of poetry may, gaining luminous transparency by their intrinsic value, transcend their immediate reference. The prophet declares the future. He does not discuss it or disclose it. *Post eventum* the words of prophecy gain referents. Yet the prophecy is not merely fulfilled. Its polyvalent verse illumines and dignifies the prophesied events.

In the first chapter we saw how, for the philosopher, "that" (τὸ ὅτι) and "why" (τὸ διὰ τί) coincide.[15] So it is also for the prophet: "In fact, it is not for the diviner to tell the 'because' (τὸ διότι) but only the 'that' (τὸ ὅτι); his art is a reading of letters written in nature." (3.3 [48].6.17–19). In the first chapter, we discussed the example of the ox and its horns. The horns of the Form of ox would exist not for defense but for completion of its essence.[16] If we were to adapt this example to the present discussion, we would then say that to know that the ox has horns in order to be an ox is to know the "that" of the ox, to declare its "oxness." Such knowledge is fore-knowledge (πρόνοια) in the sense that the animal is known before, or independently of, any causal sequence of events that might produce it. The essence exists before any feature that would safeguard it in this world and the cause was absorbed into the essence (οὐσία ἦν καὶ πρὶν τοῦτο, 6.7 [38].3.17–18). The prophet also has knowledge independent of causal sequences. In so far as philosophy shares with prophecy acts that declare such knowledge, it too can be called mantic. Prior knowledge of its "thatness" illumines for us the ox known in our sense experience. We are able to see it, as in a frame, detached from the soteric web of causality in which it has horns only for defence. Even so does the language of prophecy illumine and enhance the events that it predicts once these have happened.

What could it mean to say that philosophical language may declare the One? Declaration need not exclude discussion. Indeed, if it is philosophical language that declares the One, then the language of declaration must rather embrace the language of discussion. What

15. Cf. 6.7 [38].2.1–11 and pp. 17–18 above.
16. p. 18 and 6.7. [38].10.1–2.

would it mean to discuss the One in such a way that we also declare it?

Plotinus discusses the presence of the One to Intellect in illuminationist language (6.7 [38].22). The beauty (κάλλος) of Intellect is dormant until it receives the light of the One.[17] The One in the act of illumination confers grace (χάριτας δόντος, line 7) upon the Forms. The word "grace" (χάρις) may, as Hadot observes,[18] be taken both in the classical Hellenic sense of the grace of beauty and in the Christian theological sense of gift without condition. A wonderful illustration is provided:[19] "If [the soul] remains in Intellect, it sees many beautiful (*kala*) and august things, but it does not yet have that which it seeks. It is as if it approaches a face which, while beautiful, may yet not excite vision, in which there is not conspicuous a diffusion of grace (χάρις ἐπιθέουσα)" (lines 21–24). Plotinus proceeds to argue that beauty consists, not in symmetry or proportion, but in the beauty that shines upon symmetry in spiritual illumination.[20] Thus the face of a corpse may have symmetry and yet lack the beauty of a living countenance (lines 26–29).[21]

In the next chapter Plotinus says:[22] "There indeed, that which the soul pursues and which bestows light upon Intellect and the trace which fell from it and is stirring – we should not be amazed if it has such a great power, drawing to itself [the soul] and summoning (ἀνακαλουμένου) it from all wandering, so that it [the soul] may find its repose in disposition toward itself [i.e. the One]" (6.7 [38].23.1–4). Plato in the *Cratylus* derives *kalon* ("beautiful") from *kalein* ("to call").[23] Plotinus, in his use of *anakaleisthai* ("summon"), doubtless intends the Platonic etymology.[24] This suggests that beauty may be a call, or word, from the One which summons us toward itself in a moment of illumination and grace.

Plotinus gives voice to the cosmos' declaration of its creator: "Looking upon it one might readily hear from it, 'A god made me,'" (3.2

17. 6.7 [38].22.11–12.
18. Hadot, *Plotin ou la Simplicité du regard*, 65–68
19. My translation.
20. 6.7 [38].22.24–29.
21. Cf. 1.6 [1].1.37–40.
22. My translation.
23. 416d4–10
24. Cf. Lewy, *Chaldaean Oracles*, 439.

[47].3.19–21). This passage seems to be reflected in St Augustine's powerful phrase: *Ecce sunt caelum et terra, clamant, quod facta sint.*[25] Speech as declaration is located, not only in ourselves, but in the cosmos of which we speak. We bring it to articulation. As the word is not just our project but part of creation as a whole, we need not read this passage merely in terms of the literary device of personification. As Intellect creates the world, its icon, the creation, speaks to us of Intellect and (indirectly) Intellect thus speaks to us, summoning us to itself.

Plotinus also says that: "Indeed this cosmos exists through him [the One] and each and every god and all that depends from him prophesies (προφητεύει) to men and proclaims what is dear to them" (2.9 [33].9.39–42). In this prophecy, the cosmos in its beauty and order declares the One.[26]

We may resume our discussion of 6.7 [38].23. Plotinus reasons:[27] "The other things that they say are goods (λέγουσιν ἀγαθά) [they say are such] with reference to this [i.e., the Good], but they say that this is good with reference to nothing [of these]" (lines 17–18). Here we have again the problem of 5.3 [49].14 that language, since it proceeds from sequents of the One, may not disclose the One. Plotinus continues: "What then does such a principle create? Indeed it created mind, it created life, souls are from this [principle] and all other things which participate in language (*logos*) or intelligence, or life" (lines 18–20).[28] The One is also described as "inspiring mind, inspiring life" (lines 23–24). Here we have, as in 5.3 [49].14, the notion that speech is itself a part of creation.

In 6.7 [38].22 and 23 we are presented with three senses of *legein*, "to say": Disclosure, discussion, and declaration. As in 5.3 [49].14, discussion will not of itself yield disclosure. Yet language is a part of creation and as such a gift of the One.

25. *Confessions* xi and Perler, *Der Nus bei Plotin*, 22–23 and 23 note 1.

26. The verb προφητεύειν is not used elsewhere in Plotinus. Cf. Phillips, "The Universe as Prophet," 276–81, who shows how this passage addresses Gnostic claims to divine origins by asserting that contemplation of the cosmos, viewed as a unity, is a necessary propaedeutic to the ascent of the soul to the One. This passage also contains a lower level of prophecy in which, in contemplation of the multiplicity of the cosmos, the stars and planets reveal the "interrelationship of all aspects of the sense world." (Phillips, 278).

27. My translation.

28. My translation.

We may see the function of language as declaration in the notion that beauty may call or summon us to the One from which it descends. The beauty of the Forms may, in an act of illumination, grace, and transcendence declare the One. Even so may our words, charged with divine energy, become speech about and from the One, declaring the first principle and summoning us toward it.

In 6.9 [9].7 Plotinus speaks of how the soul, in union with the One, must abandon sense, form, and self in its vision of the One and:

Having come together with it and sufficiently, so to speak, having achieved communion with it, should go forth and proclaim, if it may, to another the association which it had there. It was with respect to such [an association] that Minos, who was famed to have become the familiar of Zeus, recalling it [that association] established the laws, as images of it, having been filled by contact with the divine unto the institution of laws. (lines 21–26)[29]

Obviously the laws of Minos are cast in words and yet they are not simply a product of his own deliberative or discursive thought. They also declare his contact with Zeus. Theological discussion is similarly not simply a product of discursive thought. It also reflects divine contact as it declares the One, even if it may not disclose the One.

Plotinus compares[30] the Forms in Intellect with the ideogrammatic symbols on Egyptian temple walls:[31] "Inscribing in their temples one particular image of one particular thing, they manifested the non-discursiveness of the intelligible world, that is that every image is a kind of knowledge and wisdom and is a subject of statements, all together in one and not discourse or deliberation" (5.8 [31].6.6–9). It is only later that this unity of vision is divided in discursive script and discourse.[32]

Yet language exists at the level of Intellect. Thus "all of the things that are said there are beautiful images" (5.8 [31].5.21–22). Plotinus supposes that the Intellect might say, "I am being." In this case, the very structure of the sentence, containing as it does both subject and predicate, would indicate multiplicity as identity in difference and

---

29. My translation. Plotinus is here thinking of the association of Minos with Zeus in Plato, *Laws* 624a1-b3.

30. 5.8 [31].5.20 – 6.15.

31. See de Keyser, *Signification de l'art*, 60–62.

32. 5.8 [31].6.9–12.

implies both being and thought.[33] If the One, however, were to say, "I am this," it would, by the use of a predicate introduce an inadmissible difference and manyness. Even to say "am am" or "I I" would suggest the copula and multiplicity.[34]

In 6.9 [9].7 speech as declaration is preceded by vision[35] or contact.[36] Thus speech as declaration reflects experience. There is always in Plotinus a triadic structure of tradition, reason, and experience.[37] He never makes an authoritarian, mystical appeal to experience at the expense of reason. We have also seen that the inability of speech to disclose the One does not allow us to forego discussion. The very status of speech as a gift from the One carries with it the imperative of theological discourse.

The present study has argued that Plotinus uses two models of discourse when he discusses the relations between the intelligible and the sensible world: the models of representation and reflection. In representation we analyse and divide the intelligible subject very much as an artist might resolve the attributes of his subject into discrete qualities which in their aggregate – in the painting – may display an appearance of unity. Representation is a useful model to the philosopher who seeks to understand the intelligible world in terms of the relations of participation and likeness which exist between the intelligible and sensible worlds. Plotinus counterbalances the language of representation with the language of reflection. The latter stresses the

33. 5.3 [49].13.21–28.
34. 5.3 [49].10.35–37; cf. 6.7 [38].38.14–25: The Good may not say, "I am the Good." See Beierwaltes, *Denken des Einen*, 102–3; cf. Beierwaltes, *Platonismus und Idealismus* 22, 45, 69, and 152 on 5.3 [49].10.37 "εἰμὶ εἰμὶ" καὶ "ἐγὼ ἐγώ." Beierwaltes reads this passage as an anticipation of the Hegelian speculative statement in which the predicate does not add to or qualify the subject; rather the subject and predicate stand to each other in a reflexive, dynamic, and dialectical relationship. The absence of the relative pronoun in Plotinus' hypothetical sentences here is interesting. Beierwaltes studies the history of effect of this passage in later Neoplatonism, mediaeval philosophy, and German idealism. The higher souls, before the descent into body, make no use of discursive reasoning, but do enjoy a kind of silent and intuitive communication, cf. 4.3 [27].18 and Theiler, *"Die Sprache des Geistes,"* 305–7; Theiler locates this idea in the history of ancient theories of language. While the thought of Intellect is non-discursive, this does not mean that it need be non-propositional, cf. Sorabji, "Myths," *pace* Lloyd, "Non-discursive thought."
35. 6.9 [9].7.20: θέα.
36. 6.9 [9].7.25: ἐπαφῇ.
37. See Armstrong, "Tradition, Reason and Experience."

continuity of sensible with intelligible reality and the real presence of
the intelligible in the sensible world. The colour in a mirror image is
a projection of an attribute which really is in the model and is continuous with that attribute.

What I am arguing here is that speech, as its various sensible referents, itself belongs to the creation. All of speech, whether it employs
the model of representation or of reflection, is not merely an instrument, but is itself a created thing. As such, it may, as may any other
created thing, either describe or reflect the One. In its aspect as declaration, language may be said to reflect the One as it is charged with
real presence and establishes continuity with its creator.[38]

Even as speech as declaration is a gift from above, so is speech as
discussion. In the passage concerning the Egyptian ideogrammatic
symbols[39] we have seen how, on Plotinus' view, the priests proceeded
from the ideogrammatic symbols that communicated the immediacy
of intuitive vision to cursive script that expressed discursive thought.
There is a movement from intuition to discursive speech or a transition from vision, touch, and experience generally to language. Plotinus sees an inborn deficiency in the soul. It can never be content to
achieve unity with its object of contemplation, but must always step
back and see it as other, examining it in discursive thought and speech
(3.8 [30].6.21–25).[40] Our knowledge of the Intellect comes from Intellect itself, or from what source would we derive our capacity to
discuss it (λέγειν περὶ αὐτοῦ, 5.3 [49].8.41–44)? As (in the preceding
lines 36–41) Intellect is said to see itself as light by means of light,
Plotinus must mean that it is accessible to us also as light, i.e., as both
means and object of vision. Plotinus here implies that speech as discussion is a gift to us from Intellect, as is precisely the knowledge of
itself given to us by Intellect the *sine qua non* of such discussion. If we
see intuition as giving birth to speech and speech as the attempt to
recapture intuition, then we must surely see the relation between
intuition and speech as dialectical. If declaration belongs to the moment of vision, then discussion must have the immediacy of declaration as its goal. Thus the relationship between declaration and
discussion must also be dialectical.

38. For my differences with the position of Crome, *Symbol und Unzulänglichkeit* on
the nature of language in Plotinus, see Schroeder, "Saying and Having," 82–84
    39. 5.8 [31].5–6.
    40. Cf. de Keyser, *Signification de l'art,* 63–64.

To understand this, let us imagine a very good conversation. We analyse and divide our subject with all the weapons of discursive reason. Suddenly, if the conversation is indeed a fine one, we may feel that we have transcended ourselves in a moment of deepening understanding and intuition. Yet that very intuition, after a moment of silence, reflection, excitement, and enjoyment may give birth to yet other discourse as it in turn is analysed and considered discursively. This is a model of philosophizing which will remain unpopular with those who see philosophy as a matter of nailing down ideas or providing definitive statements. For those who see such conversation as a continuing fusion of horizons, the Plotinian dialectic of intuition and language will be more welcome.[41]

In 3.8 [30].6, Plotinus asserts that the soul, when united with its object of contemplation, is in a condition of silence or quiet (ἡσυχίαν ἄγει, line 12). Yet if the soul is not full, i.e., not in this condition of union, it will utter speech about that object and so distance itself from that object. Even then, however, there is a sense in which the soul sees in silence what it utters (ὁρᾷ μέντοι καὶ αὐτὴ ἡσύχως ἃ προφέρει). The soul is attempting through examination to understand what it has (καταμανθάνουσα ὃ ἔχει).[42]

In this passage the relationship between saying and having which we have examined in other texts is also at work. The "saying" here is a discussion of what the soul "has" imperfectly. Its end is to secure a surer union with the object of its contemplation that will consist in the "having" of ecstasy and contemplation.

If there is in this passage a dialectical relationship between intuition and language and if, further, intuition is a function of silence, then the relationship between word and silence must also be dialectical. If the language of discussion attempts to understand the immediacy of intuitive experience and indeed to return the soul to that intuitive moment, then we are surely invited to see in Plotinian philosophy intelligence in the defence of innocence.[43]

---

41. Cf. Beierwaltes, "Image and Counterimage," 245: "Even the *language of Neoplatonic philosophy* shows a fundamental anti-dogmatic trait."

42. 3.8. [30].6.21–29.

43. Cf. Charles-Saget, *L'Architecture du Divin*, 101: "Ainsi, la parole vivante joue sans cesse entre différents niveaux. Et il serait trop simple de l'opposer au silence comme à son contraire. *Le silence est son centre*."

Plato, in the *Seventh Letter*[44] says of the highest reality that he shall never write a treatise concerning it and that it is ineffable. Plotinus construes this statement to refer to the One. Yet, says Plotinus, "We speak and write impelling toward it" (λέγομεν καὶ γράφομεν πέμποντες εἰς αὐτό).[45] We have seen[46] how, in our speech declaring the One, we may "have toward" (ἔχειν πρὸς) the One. What is the force of the prepositions εἰς and πρός in these passages? Let us take the One as an object which transcends speech. While we may not disclose the One in the sense of making it utterly transparent in speech, we may yet direct the penetrating ray of regard toward it. While our speech uses images of one sort or another, or our awareness constructs or is presented with images of the One that would veil it from us, still we direct our regard not toward images of the One but towards itself.

Discussion and declaration are not acts that occur, as it were, independently of each other. Sometimes we discuss, at other times we declare. We argued that on a proper understanding declaration may be an exalted moment of discussion. We should rather say that all discussion should be declarative with respect to its intentionality.

If we say that the One is an object of interpretation, then we must entertain the hypothesis that it shares the generic characteristics of interpretation. Interpretation requires a hermeneutical distance from the text or other object that we seek to interpret. We approach a book from the horizon of our experience, personal, linguistic, and historical. As the horizon of each one of us is different, we shall offer different interpretations of the same text. The bible in English will be quite different from the bible in French or German. This is not to say that there are not agreements and commonalities among them. Even a translation is not a mere transcription, but an interpretation. There is scarcely a more foolish phrase than "definitive interpretation."

Despite these limitations, an interpretation must seek, as its ultimate goal, as its paradigm, however unapproachable, the coincidence of its horizon with the horizon of the text. Indeed the interpreter is himself invaded and interpreted by the text as his own language begins to assume its idioms (e.g., the Hebrism "king of kings" in bible translation) or as his own moral and spiritual being is challenged. Without

---

44. 341c4–5.
45. 6.9 [9].4.12–13.
46. 5.3 [49].14.13.

the attempt to know the text in spirit and in life, the interpretation will become a dead letter. Yet the text is vivified not by some one "definitive" act of decoding, but in the free play of an interpretation in which the interpreter recognizes his own horizons.

If we read Plotinus without an appropriate hermeneutical approach, we may receive a sad picture of the progress of the soul. The weary soul, having attained the end of its journey, unable to abide in union with the One, will descend yet again into the world of sense. The talk of ascent and descent of the soul may be as boring as the doctrine of "emanation" and the dull topography of his intelligible universe. Yet it comes to life if we strip it of inherited mythical paradigms[47] and attempt to see for ourselves what hermeneutic, what living dialectical process it is, that Plotinus is attempting to construct.

The soul, upon its "ascent" to the One, speaks, in the sense that it declares the One.[48] Why, in this moment of intuition, does it trouble to declare the One? Why not simply abide in light and silence? We must recall that the source, on the model of reflection, projects its image externally, whether or not there is a reflective surface which may image it. The source also contains that image and the activity of imaging intrinsically. Now the word of declaration is a reflected image of the source. It is projected extrinsically, but is also contained intrinsically in the source. Therefore the soul, by its very union with the source, must join in the act of declaration. That declaration is also projected extrinsically, i.e., the soul becomes an instrument of that extrinsic projection by the very fact of union.

Now the declaration, (e.g., "I have seen") is open to interrogation ("*What* have you seen?"). Suppose it is answered, "What I have seen is not *a* what." We are here already involved in interpretation. If there is some descended part of me left to resume the question, I may be reduced to the act of interpretation and the completion of the circle, which itself began in the sensible world and the realm of discursive thought. Even if there is no such descended part (and at death I am utterly whole and purified) I have still engaged in the projection of the what-is-said of declaration which may be taken up by others, thus

47. Indeed for Plotinus himself, myth, including Platonic myth, has the purpose of separating out in time and space entities to which these categories do not truly apply (3.5 [50].9.24–29).

48. 6.9 [9].7.21–23.

initiating for humanity (descended humanity) the resumption of the hermeneutical circle.

Union with the One may be conceived as an act of perfect congruence: with the whole of ourselves we embrace and coincide with the whole of the One. Or we may think that only some small part of the soul is engulfed in the One. Yet we need not be confined to these alternatives. Congruence may be the goal of our quest, even if it is never perfectly achieved, just as total comprehension may be the end of interpretation, even though a surplus of meaning yet remains. The goal is necessary to the interpretive process, even though it may only be glimpsed speechlessly in the wonderful moment of intuition when we surrender our thoughts and questions to the enjoyment of the object of interpretation.

Plotinus expresses the goal of congruence in saying that we should abandon this world "that we might with the whole of ourselves (τῷ ὅλῳ αὐτῶν) embrace [the One] and have no part with which we do not touch God" (6.9 [9].9.54–55). Yet the intended congruence remains unachieved. Thus Plotinus asks: "How does one not abide there? Indeed because he did not come out [from this world] whole" (6.9 [9].10.1–2). I prefer to render ὅλος here as "whole" in preference to Armstrong's "totally," both because the word is adjectival rather than adverbial in form and because it makes the point that the goal of congruence remains unrealized.

In the previous chapter, Plotinus says that we should abandon this world "that we might with the whole of ourselves (τῷ ὅλῳ αὐτῶν) embrace [the One] and have no part with which we do not touch God" (6.9 [9].9.54–55). When the soul is detached from this world, its address to the One may (in a phrase familiar even to those with a slender acquaintance with Plotinus) be called "the flight of the alone to the alone" (φυγὴ μόνου πρὸς μόνον).[49] The word "alone" (μόνος) signifies a freedom from external and social attachments, a transcendence of all plurality, all dialogue, and even all internal relationships.[50] Still, it is not the case that some isolated fragment of the soul is engulfed in the One. The union with the One belongs to our integrity.

Plotinus does (6.9 [9].10) entertain the possibility that perfect union in the sense of congruence with the One may be realized in the future,

49. 6.9 [9].11.51.
50. Cf. Trouillard, "Valeur critique," 431–44 and 1.4 [46].10.30 and 1.6 [1].7.9.

i.e., after death.[51] Yet now, from our merely partial vision, we are drawn back to demonstration, evidence, and dialectic.[52] Even so the act of partial vision was greater than speech, as was its object.[53]

Union with the One has as its limiting case perfect congruence. Our concern here is with the function of the word for use by mortal seekers as indeed it is with the word of Plotinus at work in his seminar. The One is infinite: it cannot be embraced or be comprehended in the sense of perfect congruence (ἄπειρον – τῷ ἀπεριλήπτῳ τῆς δυνάμεως, 6.9 [9].6.10–12). It is in this failure of comprehension that the soul will again examine in word and speech the content of its vision.[54]

In the first chapter, we saw how Plotinus interprets Platonic *anamnêsis* not as a temporal recollection of Forms seen in a past life but as an extra-temporal engagement of our consciousness which may be actualized at the level of our waking consciousness.[55] We saw this interpretation as an incipient demythologization of Plato. O'Daly[56] remarks: "Strictly speaking his critique would make pre-existence irrelevant to the theory in which *anamnêsis* is reduced to a realization of the mind's consubstantiality with its objects. Philosophically irrelevant, that is: but for Plotinus, who wanted only to be the interpreter of the master, Plato (V 1,8,10 ff.), an impossibility reconciled with piety." In the present chapter, we shall see how Plotinus' understanding of this topic renders the experience of intelligible reality more comprehensible in humane terms. In the final chapter, we shall seek

51. 6.9 [9].10.2–3.
52. 6.9 [9].10.4–7.
53. 6.9 [9].10.7–9.
54. I do not wish, for the purposes of this book, to enter into elaborate discussion of all the texts that describe the union of the soul with the One. A good review of relevant texts is to be found in Seidl, "L'union mystique," who distinguishes epistemological, psychological/mystical, and ontological accounts of the union and argues that there is an ontological union as between formal and material causes (as in Aristotle). In view of the formless and indeterminate character of Form in Plotinus (see pp. 62–64 above), this conclusion would seem incorrect. Arguing for unity rather than identity, Seidl concludes that the soul is neither absorbed into the One nor annihilated in the union. I would prefer to say that the union is hermeneutical and existential in character. The union should be seen, not as formation, but as transformation which continues to affect the soul after its descent. The account of the union in Plotinus is, of course, very rich, including descriptive, instructive, and philosophical elements, cf. Miller, "Union with the One."
55. pp. 11–12.
56. O'Daly, "Memory in Plotinus," 469

to examine how that experience may be not only humane but communal. The doctrine of reincarnation or of final delivery from its wheel leads to a narrow ontology of soul and its objects that, I shall maintain, limits our understanding of the true meaning of union with the divine in Plotinus. This is not to deny that these burjdensome elements of ontology are present in our author.[57] Yet as Armstrong properly remarks,[58] "He [Plotinus] is much less concerned and excited than most Christians, and indeed most Platonists, about life after death because he is so confident that he can live in his heaven, the world of Intellect, and attain to union with God while still in the body and this world." Perhaps it would be best to carry the Plotinian demythologization of *anamnêsis* a step further and not pay too much attention to life before birth or after death.

Plotinus argues that the noetic activity of the soul may be impeded when it is brought to reflective awareness. Thus, the reader may read more successfully when he is not aware that he is reading, a man is more brave when unconscious of his bravery (and so with other examples).[59] Plotinus employs the word *parakolouthêsis* that may describe a self-conscious awareness which may impede activity.[60]

Let us suppose that I am at the summer cottage on a rainy afternoon. I ask myself what I shall do. I shall read a book, let us say, *Treasure Island*. At first I am aware of taking the book down from the shelf, making myself comfortable, turning the pages, and attempting to concentrate. If the effort is successful, these actions and their environment will be relegated to the halo of awareness as my regard is focussed on the fantastic contents of the book, on Long John Silver and the parrot. I may say that I am "at one with" the story.

This act of reading seems replete with innocence. That it is not innocent will be revealed only when I undertake to discuss the book with a companion who has also read it. This is to say that our interpretations of the book will differ. Thus the supposedly innocent act of reading will be shown, after all, to be an act of interpretation. That task of interpretation proceeds from the horizon of my experience, my memory, and my history. The book has its own horizon, the ho-

57. For reincarnation in Plotinus, see 3.4 [15].2; 6.7 [38].6–7; 3.2 [47].13 and Armstrong, "Form, Individual and Person," 62–63; cf. Rich, "Reincarnation in Plotinus."
58. "Form, Individual and Person," 66.
59. 1.4 [46].10.21–33.
60. Cf. 2.9 [33].1.43; 4.4 [28].4.10; 1.4 [46].9.15.

rizon, e.g., of the period of history in which it was written. The act of reading involves a fusion of horizons which will differ from reader to reader and from one historical epoch to another. The act of reading will also embrace the moments of intuition and immediacy, on the one hand, and of analysis and the attempt to recapture immediacy, on the other. This process is not a wanton to and fro. In its avoidance of closure, it constitutes an ever fruitful opening of horizons.

Plotinus observes:[61] "Sense-perception is our messenger, but Intellect is our king. But we too are kings, when we are in accord with it; we can be in accord in two ways, either by having something like its writing written in us like laws, or by being filled with it and able to see it and be aware of it as present" (5.3 [49].3.44 − 4.4). Plotinus continues:

If, therefore, it [the part that reasons discursively] says that it is from Intellect and second after Intellect and an image of Intellect, having in itself everything as if written [in it], as the one who writes and has written in there [in Intellect], will one who knows himself as far as this stop there, but shall we by using another power as well behold also the Intellect which knows itself, or, having a part in that Intellect, since that too belongs to us and we belong to it, shall we in this way know Intellect and ourselves? (4.20–27)

With sense-perception we read the great book of nature and reflexively read ourselves. Yet our textuality is the creation of Intellect. This very reflection begins to place us within the horizon of the author (as implicit in his cosmic text). Again the dialectical tension between speech and vision is realized as we behold (κατόψομεθα, line 25) Intellect. It is in sharing the vision of Intellect that we enter into identity with it and belong to it as it belongs to us. We may again think of the ineffable contact of Minos the lawgiver with Zeus.[62] The text as seen from the horizon of Intellect will consist in those transparent symbols of the Egyptians that express the non-discursive thought of Intellect.[63]

Plotinus observes: "So we also possess the forms in two ways, in our souls in a manner of speaking unfolded (ἀνειλιγμένα) and separated,

61. The reference is to Plato *Philebus* 28c7–8 where intellect is said to be king of heaven and earth. Some of the material in square brackets is supplied by Armstrong and some by myself.

62. 6.9 [9].7.23–26.

63. 5.8 [31].6.5–7.

in Intellect all together" (1.1 [53].8.6–8).[64] The verb ἀνελίττω ("unroll") can refer to the opening of a scroll[65] and, by extension, to the act of reading or interpreting.[66] Whether Plotinus intends either the sense of revelation (implicit in unrolling), or of reading or interpretation, we may see that the Platonic Forms as immanent in the world possess the sort of textuality ascribed to sense perception in 5.3 [49].4. We read the cosmic text that is Intellect "unrolled" into the sensible world. In so doing we trace or follow the discursive analysis and division of what in Intellect is noetic unity. However, the final goal of such interpretation is an act of total comprehension.

Plotinus describes the soul's ascent to the One in terms of a person entering a temple, seeing many images of the god and then, upon entering the innermost shrine, seeing, not a statue or image of the god, but the god itself (αὐτό). Then he qualifies. The One is, not an object of vision (θέαμα), but another way of seeing (ἄλλος τρόπος τοῦ ἰδεῖν).[67]

In another passage Plotinus compares the address of the soul to the One to a man who enters a great house and admires its furnishings and appointments.[68] The visitor then sees the master of the house, whom he judges to be truly worthy of his contemplation and, concentrating his gaze upon him, he blends his vision with the object of vision, so that what was formerly an object of vision (ὁρατὸν) becomes vision (ὄψις).[69] Plotinus describes the encounter with the master of the house as later in time than our admiration of his household. Had we seen the master and the appointments of his house simultaneously, we might not have attended to the master himself until we had fully absorbed our surroundings. The temporal sequence intends only to show that, when we do see the master, we behold him as the recapitulation and unifying principle of the environment he has himself created, not just as something else to see. The vision of the master in his house means that we alter our way of seeing because we now understand the house as an expression of his artistic tastes and accomplishments.

---

64. Cf. 4.3 [27].5.10: the souls are more unrolled (ἐξειλιγμέναι) than the intellects to which they are attached.

65. Aristotle *Problemata* xvi.6.914a27.

66. Xenophon *Memorabilia* i.6.14; Plato *Philebus* 15e3.

67. 6.9 [9].11.17–23.

68. 6.7 [38].35.7–16.

69. Cf. 1.6 [1].8.25–26; 9.22–23.

Vision of the One is iconoclastic; it destroys our images of it. This is the very formlessness that, as we saw in the previous chapter, so terrifies the soul.[70] The sunrise of the One overwhelms our horizon, our interpretive activities that would limit the One.[71] In this sense the One interprets us. What does it mean that the One for us becomes, not an icon, but vision, another way of seeing? Again, we may appeal to our example of reading. Do we not say that the study of a text may alter our vision, our way of looking? In this case, it is not simply that such study presents us with new and curious things to look at, that we may, from our horizon, interpret them. Rather the text invades our horizon and interprets us, changes our way of looking.

The act of intuiting the One in union is not as innocent as the example of unimpeded and unselfconscious reading might suggest. I am transported into the wonder world of *Treasure Island,* with no barriers between myself and the story. However, as we have seen, reading itself is not innocent. My barriers are being invaded. And as I step back from the act of union which conveyed that sense of immediacy, I find that I also have, from my horizon, contributed to that experience. If we see the act of intuition as not wholly innocent of interpretation, then we must see in the union of the soul with the One some contribution of the soul from the horizon of its own experience. Even the command that we put away all things (ἄφελε πάντα)[72] need not exclude some purified residuum of personality and experience from the moment of union.

In archaic Greece, human identity was construed as a person's life, his *bios,* as a passive unfolding of destiny culminating in an Apollonian self-knowledge and humility (*sôphrosunê*). The Socrates of Plato and Xenophon challenges this view by understanding the sense of *bios* as a Heraklean and humanistic self-assertion. In the care of the soul, the care of oneself, humanity itself chooses the path of life that it will lead. As human identity is progressively identified with the rational soul, the link between felicity and external goods and life experience is severed. The wise man may be happy even upon the rack.[73]

Plotinus may also appear to reflect this tradition of discounting the importance of biography in favour of the progress of the rational soul

---

70. Cf. 6.9 [9].3.1–6 and p. 62.
71. 5.5 [32].8.1–16 and pp. 45–47.
72. 5.3 [49].17.38.
73. Cf. Schroeder, "The Self in Ancient Religious Experience."

in the intelligible world. Of interest here is his interpretation of a passage in the *Odyssey* of Homer:[74]

Next I saw the strength of Herakles,
An image (εἴδωλον); but he himself (αὐτὸς)
    with the immortal gods
Rejoices in abundance and his slender-footed Hebe,
The child of great Zeus and Hera of the golden sandals.

This passage offers a great contrast with Homer's usual view of the soul as a dull and sorrowful shade. There is a long and fruitful tradition of interpretation of it on the part of those concerned with the mysteries of human identity.[75] Plotinus understands the image of Herakles to be the lower soul in the role of Herakles as historical figure and Herakles himself (*autos*) to be the rational soul.[76] He asks whether the higher soul will have memory of friends, children, wife, or fatherland? The lower soul remembers these objects with passion, but the higher soul retains these memories passively.[77] Herakles in heaven holds these in slight regard. Yet a further Herakles, this time translated to the realm of the Plotinian Intellect will, in rapt contemplation of the Forms, not have these memories.[78]

Memory would seem crucial to human identity. Yet we may ask, could Herakles, in rapt contemplation of the Forms, not retain something of his human formation? After all, if the Plotinian Herakles is to be true to the Herakles of myth and literature, he must be truly man as well as truly god.[79] At the level of the higher soul, wife, children, and fatherland were reduced to marginal objects of awareness as Herakles gained a new theme and focus of consciousness in the Platonic Forms. Now that his former objects of affection have

---

74. xi.601–4.

75. The passage is doubtless a later addition to the text of Homer. Its philosophical exegesis may have originated in the Old Academy or in post-Platonic Pythagoreanism, cf. Pépin, "Héraklès et son Reflet," 187–92.

76. 6.4 [22].16.36–48; 1.1 [53].12.31–39 and Pépin, "Héraklès et son Reflet," 174–76.

77. 4.3 [27].32.1–4; cf. 4.3 [27].27.

78. 4.3 [27].32.24 – 4.4 [28].1.1–11; and Schroeder, "The Self in Ancient Religious Experience," 354–55.

79. Cf, Pindar *Nemean Odes* 3.39 (Herakles as ἥρως θεός) and Wilamowitz, *Euripides Herakles* vol. 1:38; Shapiro, "Heros Theos."

receded, we need not think that Herakles has become an amorphous soul with no character of its own.

Memory is added to the soul (or actualized in it) upon its descent (4.4 [28].3). Plotinus reflects[80] that when the soul descends, it has the object of its desire in proportion to its memory and imaging power. Yet when we speak of memory in this context, we are not to think of it as belonging to the awareness that one is remembering. It may consist rather in the soul's being disposed toward its previous experiences. When the soul brings the fact of remembrance to awareness, it sinks even lower. Our knowledge of the objects of memory may be even stronger when unimpeded by awareness that we have them. Here again Plotinus summons the notion of *parakolouthêsis*[81] to demonstrate the superiority of unreflected awareness.

Plotinus then reasons that, if the soul upon her descent recovers memories of what she has seen, she must have had them, in some sense, there too before her descent. The soul had memories, but potentially. The actuality of the intelligible objects of contemplation obscured these memories. Upon her descent, the soul actualizes these memories as it sees the same things it saw before its ascent.

In the following chapter (4.4 [28].5), Plotinus reflects that the power of memory is continuous with the same power by which we see the intelligible Forms. Thus memory may anagogically lead us back to the primal vision of the Forms. Plotinus observes:

For one must not, when one makes statements about the intelligible world, use analogy or syllogistic reasoning which takes its principles from elsewhere, but even when we are here below we can speak about the intelligible realities by that same power which is able to contemplate the higher world. For one must see the things in that world by a kind of awakening of the same power, so that one can awake it in that higher world also; as if one went up some high viewpoint and raising one's eyes saw what no-one saw who had not come up with one. (4.4 [28].5.5–11)

Notice that the speech of declaration here is a function of memory in which our conversation leads us back to our primary experience of Form. Plotinus asserts[82] that the soul may speak of its experience

80. 4.4 [28].4.
81. 4.4 [28].4.10.
82. 6.7 [38].34.28–35.

of the One after its descent and know that it is speaking truly. Hadot
remarks:[83] "Mais la fusion avec le Bien n'annihile pas le moi, puisque
l'âme se convient, après l'union, d'avoir reconnu celui qu'elle cher-
chait." This is surely a more secure argument for the preservation of
human identity in the union than are the ontological arguments based
upon geometrical imagery that we discussed above.

   If we can, upon our descent, remember the Forms, can we also,
upon our ascent, remember things here? It was suggested by Plotinus
in the previous chapter (4.4 [28].4) that such memories were latent
and potential when we saw the Forms. We have also seen that Herakles, at the level of the upper soul, retains passive memories of his
past.[84] Now Plotinus tells us that we may recognize people from our
terrestrial life, if not from their astral bodies, then from "their character and the individuality of their behaviour."[85] Indeed, if they could
talk, they would also recognize each other from their conversation.[86]
Indeed Plotinus does state elsewhere that the higher souls enjoy a
silent form of communication in the absence of discursive reasoning.[87]

   Thus memory works in two directions as we remember or recall
our experience of the Forms or as we passively remember our past
terrestrial experience or even actively recognize the souls of those
whom we have known on earth. Our conversation on earth attempts
to recapture experience of the Forms as a task of memory and of love
– love for the beyond and love for those who are with us in this quest.
The experience of the Forms is not just an experience on the part of
"the soul," as if each of us were reduced to an amorphous existence
in this moment, a soulless soul. It is surely Herakles, a character
shaped by his past life or lives who experiences them.[88]

   Further support for the view that we do not lose individuality in
our union with the One and that the experience may serve as a foun-

83. Hadot, "Structure et Thèmes," 670.
84. 4.3 [27].32.1–4.
85. 4.4 [28].5.19–21.
86. 4.4 [28].5.21–22.
87. Cf. 4.3 [27].18 and Theiler, "Sprache des Geistes," 305–7.
88. For further argument that the soul need not lose its formation from this life
upon its ascent, cf. O'Daly, "Memory in Plotinus," 462–65. In its ascent, the soul must
struggle to rid itself of memories (4.3 [27].31.13–16); nevertheless, the soul will retain
some memories, but reject *most* upon its ascent. The higher and lower souls have memories in common (27.3–4). Ultimately the higher soul, in separation from the lower
soul, will retain only those that it chooses to select (31.16–20).

dation for communal dialogue, is provided by Plotinus' use of the first person plural in describing this union. Thus we are present to the One when we have no otherness.[89] Plotinus reflects that we dance about the One in a choral dance, not always looking toward it, as to the conductor (so that we sing off key), but when we look to the One we sing beautifully.[90] Plotinus concludes: "When we do look to him, then we are at our goal and at rest and do not sing out of tune as we truly dance our god-inspired dance around him" (6.9 [9].8.43–45). It is not clear whether the singing is homophonic or polyphonic. If it is the latter and if further the movements of each dancer are not identical, then we would have further evidence of the individuality of the experience and its hermeneutical uniqueness.[91] It will also be recalled that, in 5.3 [49].14.1–3, Plotinus asks how *we* may speak about the One.[92]

Speech, as we have seen, is the gracious gift to us of the One. Theological discourse is thus not entirely our project. The One speaks in the sense that it, in its very light, abiding, and silence, gives us the instrument by which we may not only declare it, but discuss or interpret it. Interpretation must ultimately be the project of the One (although it, of course, involves no advertence on the part of the One). When, in abiding and silence, we open ourselves to the experience, the One may stand disclosed to our intuition. However, speech (although it may declare it) cannot disclose the One. Yet the soul, as the steward of *logos*, will realize distance as it brings the act of its own intuition to a distancing and self-conscious awareness. The soul will participate in the dialectical tension between intuition and speech that its first distance from its object of contemplation prefigures. The philosophical discussion of the Plotinian circle is thus a participation in this larger scheme of things.

Yet it is also the case that, in its aspect of declaration, the word transcends the instrumentality of discussion and catapults us back to the enjoyment and immediacy of intuition. The word is not merely an instrument of analysis but is itself a uniquely valuable object of enjoyment which as such leads our regard back to its author, the One.

89. 6.9 [9].8.33–35.
90. 6.9 [9].8.37–41.
91. Cf. Rist, *Road to Reality*, 227 who makes this valuable point about 6.9 [9].8.
92. Cf. 6.5 [23].10.11–12; and Gurtler, "Human Consciousness," 256: "Plotinus does not in fact refer to experience of knowledge as 'mine'; it is always '*ours*.'"

It is thus an anagogical instrument precisely in its freedom from instrumentality. Obviously the One is that wholeness which we seek to interpret. In the motion of the hermeneutical circle, we relate the particulars of awareness to that whole. Yet we also interpret that whole with reference to the particularities that express it. The motion from declaration to discussion and back to declaration also describes this circle. Although Plato says[93] that the ultimate reality cannot be expressed in writing or speech, still "We speak and write impelling towards it" (λέγομεν καὶ γράφομεν πέμποντες εἰς αὐτό, 6.9 [9].4.12–13).

While the experience of Form must have great immediacy for each of us, it is still an interpretive and hermeneutical act. Our speech, our conversation, is dialectical in that as we seek to recover the intuitive moment each of us approaches it from his own horizon, the horizon of character and shape of soul and intellect peculiar to each. That conversation is rendered meaningful by the fact that the experience of Form is, however unconsciously, an act, not only of vision, but of interpretation. The endless talk in Plotinus of the ascent and descent of the soul is dreary as long as we observe too closely the spatial and topographical conventions belonging to the architecture of his intelligible universe. When we realize that the relationship between word and intuition is dialectical and that the intuition is itself a hermeneutical act, then we may enter enthusiastically into the grand conversation of a universe of discourse that is never closed. We are further to understand that our engagement in the free play of dialectic, our enjoyment of the word, not as instrument alone, but in its intrinsic value, is mandated by the free gift of the word to us from the One.[94]

93. *Letter* VII 341c5.

94. Trouillard, "Valeur critique," and Armstrong, "Neoplatonic Valuation" both argue convincingly from the transcendence of the intelligible order by the absolute in Plotinus for an open-endedness of philosophical and religious discourse.

V

Love

PORPHYRY DESCRIBES PLOTINUS' relationship to his circle with these words: "He was present at once to himself and to others (συνῆν καὶ ἑαυτῷ ἅμα καὶ τοῖς ἄλλοις)."[1] Hadot remarks,[2] "On the subject of the philosopher's rapport with others, about his 'presence to others' of which Porphyry speaks, we find no theoretical information in the treatises of Plotinus." In the present chapter, we shall see, on the contrary, that there is abundant evidence of a theoretical background, both metaphysical and ethical, for Porphyry's statement.

The presence portrayed in Porphyry's sentence is twofold: Plotinus is present both to himself and to others. What is presence to oneself? What is presence to others? What, if any, is the relationship between these two aspects of presence? We may begin with presence to oneself, as this relationship is ostensibly more difficult to explain than presence to others. Plotinus says little of human relationships as a subject of interest in itself. However, intersubjective relationships do appear as figures of speech. He uses such figurative language to discuss the psychology of the individual. Where Plato in the *Phaedrus* has the lover sculpting the soul of his beloved,[3] such moral artistry is in Plotinus to be directed to one's own soul.[4] The appropriate relationship between higher and lower aspects in the same soul is prescribed in

---

1. *Vita Plotini* 8.19.
2. Hadot, "Neoplatonist Spirituality," 231.
3. 252d7.
4. 1.6 [1].9.13.

terms of the association between a sage and his aspiring pupil,[5] a master and his servant,[6] parent and child.[7]

Presence to oneself may then be portrayed as the harmonious relationship between two aspects, one superior, the other inferior, in the same person. This relationship may be illustrated by reference to intersubjective relationships. However, there is a further dimension to presence to oneself that does not concern the relationship between higher and lower aspects in the same soul. It has rather to do with the superior aspect of the person as considered in itself, i.e., in abstraction from its relationship to the inferior aspect.

The range of human identity is not confined to the empirical world; the ego-consciousness of man may pose itself at any point on the full scale of identity that extends from the world of sense to the One.[8] As man ascends the scale of human identity, his autonomy increases. He need not be courageous with respect to his fear of this lion, or self-controlled with respect to the temptation of that shrimp scampi. His courage is then founded in the very firmness of his unity, identity, and autarchy. His is the courage not to flee from his post in the intelligible world and depart into the otherness of the world of sense. As the Form is in unity and identity and not scattered among the particulars, so is his autarchy, unity, identity, and virtue as he identifies his self with the Form.

In 1.2 [19].6 Plotinus approaches this autarchy by distinguishing phases of human identity on this basis. The highest level is the noetic or intelligible. The lowest is the empirical or historical. Within the dynamic continuity that extends between these two extremes is a phase of identity, descended from the intelligible world and still partaking in it that may serve as a model to the empirical phase. The relation between this higher phase (descended, as Plotinus describes it, from the intelligible world) and the empirical phase is described as a relationship of master and servant. The higher phase is the master; the lower phase is the servant. Only the servant, however, is conscious of this relationship and the master is only master in relation to the servant, not *per se*.

5. 1.2 [19].5.25–27.
6. 1.2 [19].6.1–11.
7. 1.4 [46].15.15–21.
8. Cf, Dodds, "Tradition and Personal Achievement," 5 (in 1973 reprint, 135).

Plotinus introduces the relationship of master and servant as a metaphor for the relationship between higher and lower aspects of human identity in the course of a discussion of the "imitation of God" in Plato's *Theaetetus*.[9] In Plato this project is more modest in its ambition, as the imitation is qualified[10] by the words "as far as possible." As Plotinus sees the range of possible human identity extending as far as the One itself, he entertains the quest for the divinization of man:

Our concern, then, is not to be free of wrongdoing, but to be a god. If a man should be overwhelmed by an impulse contrary to his proper volition, then he would be both god and spirit, a being of double nature, or rather he would have with him (σὺν αὐτῷ) another person possessed of a different virtue – otherwise he would be a god only, although he would be among those gods who follow the First. For, on the one hand, he himself (αὐτός) is the one who came from yonder and his true nature, if it were to become such as it was at its descent, is There. On the other hand, that person with whom he lived together (συνῳκίσθη) in his descent here, that is the one whom he will render like himself (αὐτῷ ὁμοιώσει) according to the ability of that other, so that, if it is possible, that other is free from the shocks of the world, or does not perform those acts that are not pleasing to his master (δεσπότῃ). (1.2 [19].6.2–11)[11]

Here the person is said to be himself (αὐτός), both in the intelligible world before his descent, and in the intelligible world after his descent and his act of dwelling together with another person, or other phase of the soul. We may well ask whether this identity has the same status before and after its descent? Obviously it does not, if it is possible for it to be in the intelligible by becoming such as it was before its descent. Plotinus is speaking of an identity which may be located either in the intelligible world or at some point in the soul which is superior to the grade occupied by the empirical phase. In its descent it is not to be confused with that empirical self. The status of this identity, here described as "master," is more clearly revealed in its contrast with the phase with which it dwells together upon its descent. It is this phase,

9. 176b1.
10. 176b2.
11. My translation; cf. 1.2 [19].1.

described implicitly as the servant, with which the higher identity lives together in its immanence, that is to be construed as the empirical self or historical conjoint.[12]

The principle that may properly be designated as "self" (αὐτός) is in this passage also described as "master" (δεσπότης). The Greek pronoun αὐτός may, in the absence of a proper name, (like the Latin *ipse* or the Irish peasant's "himself") bear reference to the master.[13] This sense of the pronoun is here complemented by another sense, αὐτός as "same." The higher phase as master will render the lower phase as much like himself as possible (αὐτῷ ὁμοιώσει κατὰ δύναμιν, lines 9–10). Obviously the master will not *do* anything or proceed outside himself in order to accomplish this transformation. The higher principle in the soul may simply, in its abiding, serve as model.[14]

In the rest of the chapter there is a comparison between virtue in the higher and lower ranges of human identity. Virtue at the level of Intellect is not virtue but is "the act of itself and what it is" (ἐνέργεια αὐτοῦ καὶ ὅ ἐστιν). In the empirical man it is a "virtue in another which is derived from above" (τὸ ἐν ἄλλῳ ἐκεῖθεν ἀρετή, lines 12–16). The distinction is between that which is "in itself" and that which is "in another." The characteristic which inheres intrinsically in the master is appropriated in imitation as something borrowed in the servant. That which is contained enfolded in the master, residing in the master being just what he is, as an aspect of his very unity and identity, is explicated in the servant.[15]

Just as the pronoun αὐτός may, in the absence of a proper name, describe the master of a servant, so may it (again in the absence of a proper name) be used by pupils to describe their teacher or master.[16]

---

12. O'Daly, *Plotinus' Philosophy of Self*, 56, takes αὐτός (line 7) to refer to "the self, the identifiable, historical 'Socrates'" and τὸ καθ' αὐτόν (line 8) as "that principle of identity in the transcendent which corresponds to the man we know as 'Socrates' here on earth." It will be obvious that I see the contrast (as revealed by the μὲν – δὲ construction) to be between αὐτὸς μὲν – καὶ τὸ καθ' αὐτὸν (construed together) as the descended yet still higher self and ᾧ δὲ συνῳκίσθη as the empirical self or historical conjoint. See Schroeder, "Synousia, Synaisthēsis and Synesis," 696 note 52.

13. Cf. Theocritus 24.50; Aristophanes Fr.268; for its application to the great man as object of flattery, cf. Theophrastus *Characters* 2.6. Cf. Schroeder, "Synousia, Synaisthēsis and Synesis," 697 and note 53.

14. 1.2 [19].6.17: παράδειγμα.

15. Cf. Schroeder, "Synousia, Synaisthēsis and Synesis," 697.

16. Aristophanes *Clouds* 218; Plato *Protagoras* 314d3.

In 1.2 [19].5, Plotinus considers the purification of the soul. Just as the higher soul must be pure and free of passions, so must the lower soul:

The soul will be pure in all these ways and will want to make the irrational part, too, pure, so that this part may not be disturbed; or, if it is, not very much; its shocks will only be slight ones, easily allayed by the neigbourhood (γειτονήσει) of the soul: just as a man living next door to a sage (σοφῷ γειτονῶν) would profit by the sage's neighbourhood (γειτονήσει), either by becoming like him or by regarding him with such respect as not to dare to do anything of which the good man would not approve. So there will be no conflict: the presence of reason will be enough; the worse part will so respect it that even this worse part itself will be upset if there is any movement at all, because it did not keep quiet in the presence of its master (ὅτι μὴ ἡσυχίαν ἦγε παρόντος τοῦ δεσπότου), and will rebuke its own weakness. (1.2 [19].5.21–31)

Plotinus introduces the tractate, *On Virtues* (1.2 [19]), to which this passage belongs, by providing an exegesis of the passage in Plato's *Theaetetus*[17] where it is counselled that our flight from the world should consist in the imitation of God.[18] He begins the present chapter by asking after the extent of the soul's purification. When this is known, we may understand our identity (ταὐτότης) in terms of the god with whom we are to be identified.[19] The word for identity here is a substantive corresponding to the pronominal αὐτός. Thus here, as in the ensuing chapter 1.2 [19].6 (which we examined above), the question of identity is raised with the example of the master (δεσπότης). Yet here, the master is seen, not in terms of proprietary dominion, but within the relationship between the sage and his aspiring pupil. Implicitly 1.2 [19].5 invokes the pronoun referring to master in the sense of sage even as 1.2 [19].6 explicitly invokes its sense as master over servant. In both senses the dominion or instruction is exercised with no advertent act on the part of the master or teacher, who needs only serve as model for the imitation by the servant or pupil.

17. 176a-b.
18. 1.2 [19].1.
19. 1.2. [19].5.1–2.

The good pupil maintains silence (ἡσυχία) in the presence of the master,[20] doubtless because the presence of the master proceeds from silence, the silence that belongs to abiding in the intelligible world.[21]

Previous chapters of this study have shown how Plotinus responds to the introductory arguments of Plato's *Parmenides*. Plotinus' writings present us with the fruits of his deep consideration of these aporetic inquiries concerning the Platonic theory of Ideas or Forms. We can appreciate that Plotinus has thoroughly integrated his responses to their challenges in his thinking. We may further, in the passages under consideration (1.2 [19].5–6), see a reflection of the "mastership argument" in the Platonic *Parmenides*.[22]

In this passage from the *Parmenides* an aporetic consequence is derived from the assertion of the unity and identity of the Platonic Form. If each idea is "itself unto itself" (αὐτὴ καθ' αὐτὴν), then it cannot be "in us" (ἐν ἡμῖν).[23] Parmenides pursues the argument:

Therefore, whatever ideas are what they are in relation to each other, these have their essence unto themselves (αὐταὶ πρὸς αὐτὰς), but not with reference to that which is in us (πρὸς τὰ παρ' ἡμῖν), either as copy-likenesses, or however you wish to dispose them, by participation in which we severally derive our names. Those that are in us that are homonymous with those Forms again are what they are in relation to each other, but not in relation to the Forms and all things so named are named from themselves and not from the Forms.

What do you mean? said Socrates.

It is thus, said Parmenides, if someone of us is the master (δεσπότης) or servant of anyone, he is not the servant of the Form of Master or the master of the Form of Slave, but both these [relationships] are as of man to man. The Form of Mastership exists in relation to the Form of Slavery and in the same way the Form of Slavery exists in relation to the Form of Mastery, but that which is in us does not have its character with reference to them, nor do they [have their character with reference] to us, but, as I say, they exist

20. 1.2 [19].5.30.
21. For a fuller discussion of the internalization of virtue in 1.2 [19], cf. Plass, "Plotinus' Ethical Theory."
22. 133c8–134a1.
23. 133c2–4.

entirely with reference to themselves and that which is in us in the same manner in self-reference. (133c6–134a1)

Note that the Forms may not, to use Plotinian language, be defined with reference to externs. There is a sense in which, for Plotinus, this is acceptable. In 1.2 [19] Plotinus enters upon a discussion of Plato's *Theaetetus* 176b and of "imitation of God." If we imitate God by our virtue, it may be asked whether this word has the same sense when applied to God and when applied to us. God may not have the civic virtues. How can He be self-controlled where there is no fleshly temptation, or courageous where there is nothing to fear?[24]

Plotinus would not, however, agree with the premiss of the "mastership" argument, that particulars are what they are only in relationship to themselves. The relation of imitation is asymmetrical, so that, while the virtue of God exists unto itself, the externs reflect that divine virtue.[25]

In the *Phaedo*[26] Plato describes civic virtue as a mere exchange of counterfeit coins. We exercise courage in one matter, or temperance in another, only to avoid this pain, or attain that pleasure. The good man will exchange all of this currency against the one true coin of the realm. For Plotinus[27] this means that value is not measured in terms of the horizontal relations that pertain in the empirical world. Rather, value is measured by vertical relations to the world of intelligible Form in its unity, identity, and integrity. The Form is the source of justification. The sage does not look for justification to outward success, but to his secure possession intelligible virtue, exchanging for this the vain imaginings of the world.

Plotinus gives us some notion (1.2 [19].6–7) of how virtue in the intelligible world could exist as something in its own right without reference to external practice. Courage consists in immateriality and abiding (μένον) pure unto itself (ἐφ' αὑτοῦ).[28] Here we may notice that "abiding" which is used in other contexts of the internal condition of a creative source, undisturbed by its external activity of creation.

24. 1.2 [19].1.
25. 1.2 [19].2 and 7.
26. 69a-b.
27. 1.4 [46].15.
28. 1.2 [19].7.5–6.

Virtue in the intelligible world is "the act of itself, what it really is."[29] Reading this phrase in conjunction with the description of the virtue of courage as "abiding," we see an expression of the intransitive activity of the intelligible world that achieves its external expression in transitive activity proceeding to the sensible world, as heat from a flame.[30]

In the preface to the "mastership argument,"[31] Parmenides argues that if each Form exists unto itself (αὐτὴ καθ᾽ αὐτὴν), then it cannot be in us. In the "mastership argument,"[32] he says that the Forms exist in relation to themselves and not in relation to what is in us. Plotinus interprets these statements with reference to the unity and identity of the hypostasis of Intellect, which contains all Forms. Self-control does not just exist unto itself. It is the very principle of existing unto oneself (τὸ πρὸς αὐτόν). Courage does not just exist unto itself. It *is* the very principle of remaining unto oneself (τὸ ἐφ᾽ αὐτοῦ μένειν).[33] Thus the Plotinian Form not only exists in relation to itself. It *is* the very principle of existing unto oneself without the need for external reference.

The English phrase "the self" renders the pronoun a substantive. Greek cannot do that.[34] Let us stop and review our argument to this point. Plato uses the pronoun αὐτός in the predicative position to describe Form. Thus we have αὐτὸ τὸ καλόν, "beauty itself," or αὐτὸ τὸ δίκαιον, "justice itself," etc. This pronoun in the predicative position invites the translation "itself" and suggests unity and uniqueness. The same pronoun in the attributive position invites the translation "the same" and suggests identity. Plato uses the predicative position to describe Form in the introductory arguments of the *Parmenides* but the context shows that the sense of identity is also intended. For here, both the unity and the identity of the Platonic Form are at stake under the shrewd Eleatic scrutiny of the Parmenides of the dialogue.[35] Since such unity and identity cannot be found in any conceivable relation of Forms to particulars, the "mastership" argument contends that they can only be found at the level of the Forms. Plotinus locates this unity

---

29. ἐνέργεια αὐτοῦ καὶ ὅ ἐστιν, 1.2 [19].6.15.
30. Cf. 4.5 [29].7 and pp. 25–32 above.
31. *Parmenides* 133c4.
32. *Parmenides* 133c9–10.
33. 1.2 [19].7.1–6.
34. Cf. Schroeder, "The Self in Ancient Religious Experience," 336.
35. Cf. Schroeder, "The Platonic *Parmenides*."

and identity in the intelligible world and argues that it need not exist with reference to externs. Indeed any given excellence is shown not only to exist in unity and identity in the intelligible world but to *be* that unity and identity, a more profound conclusion.

Plotinus adapts his responses to the "mastership" argument, which deals with Forms and particulars, to questions of human identity. In the *Parmenides*, the Form of Master is not master in relation to human servants but in relation to the Form of Slave. Plotinus accepts the independence of this master from human servitude. He denies, however, that the phase of human identity that plays the role of master is in its own essence or in the intelligible world a master. The phase that plays the role of servant, however, is dependent upon the intelligible Master for its identity.

Porphyry, we recall,[36] described Plotinus as being present at once to himself and to others. We have now explored the sense of "presence to oneself" and have seen that it consists both in the harmonious relationship between higher and lower aspects in the same person and in the unmediated unity and identity of the superior aspect. Such radical unity and identity must be considered apart from the former kind of presence to oneself because it is of its very essence to be free from external presence or relationship. However, the two aspects of presence to oneself are related. The lower aspect of human identity may imitate and thus explicate in multiplicity the more radical unity and identity of the higher aspect. Yet the higher aspect abides what it is and is not affected or compromised by this act of imitation.

It remains to discuss what is meant by "presence to others" and whether such presence is dependent upon or derived from "presence to oneself." We have seen how Plotinus uses the imagery of master and servant or master and pupil,[37] which we would otherwise take as an intersubjective relationship, to describe the phases of an individual human identity.

For Aristotle in the *Nicomachean Ethics* self-love is the model for friendship.[38] He asks aporetically whether, if this is so, a person ought to love himself or a friend more? True self-love may fulfill the conditions required for friendship, as it will consist in the disinterested embrace of virtue (as distinct from a merely selfish embrace of external

36. See *Vita Plotini* 8.19 and p. 91 above.
37. 1.2 [19].5 and 6.
38. ix.4.1166a1–1166b29.

goods or honours). Perhaps we do not really need friends for happiness, since a truly self-sufficient man, secure in his goodness, would not require them for his fulfillment.[39]

Aristotle asks further whether the happy man needs friends at all?[40] For Aristotle the good and happy man indeed needs friends, e.g., for the exercise of beneficence,[41] justice, and temperance[42] and because of man's intrinsically social nature.[43] Since virtue is an activity and it is difficult to contemplate our own activity, we may contemplate that activity in the mirror of a friend's actions.[44]

For the purposes of understanding Plotinus, Aristotle's question whether self-love might not allow independence from friendship is more important than Aristotle's answers. Significantly Plotinus tends to internalize the language of relationship in his exploration of individual human identity, as in the example of master and servant, sage and disciple. For Aristotle the contemplative life possesses the greatest degree of autarchy since, unlike the pursuit of gain or the practice of justice, temperance, and courage, it can be practised alone and without reference to others (although even here company is preferable).[45] We practise the contemplative life not *qua* human beings but in so far as we have something divine in us.[46] Since for Plotinus all virtue proceeds from the contemplative life, intersubjective relationships are employed as figures to illustrate the inner life, as in the example of master and servant, sage and disciple. As we have seen, where Plato in the *Phaedrus*[47] has the lover sculpting the soul of his beloved, Plotinus has the lover sculpt his own soul.[48] May we nevertheless gain some knowledge of his attitude toward human relationships from these internalized examples, even though in these the relationship itself is not thematic?

39. *Nicomachean Ethics* ix.8.1168b28–1169b2.
40. *Nicomachean Ethics* ix.9.1169b3–8.
41. *Nicomachean Ethics* ix.9.1169b10–13.
42. *Nicomachean Ethics* ix.9.1169b16–19.
43. *Nicomachean Ethics* ix.9.1169b16–19.
44. *Nicomachean Ethics* ix.9.1169b30–1170a4; 1170a13-b19.
45. *Nicomachean Ethics* x.1177a27–1177b1.
46. *Nicomachean Ethics* x.1177b26–31. On the sage's need for external goods in Aristotle and its place in the ancient concept of self, see Schroeder, "The Self in Ancient Religious Experience," 352.
47. 252d7.
48. 1.6 [1].9.13.

To answer this question, we may again look to the Platonic foundations of Plotinus' position. In Plato's *Symposium*[49] the wise woman of Mantineia, after recounting the story of Poverty and Plenty, remarks: "None of the gods loves wisdom, nor does he desire to become wise – for he already is." She continues that the utterly ignorant also do not love wisdom, because they are unaware of their lack. It is only those in between these two states who love. The statement implies that eros, as evaluative love, while it may be directed by men to divine wisdom, is not be felt by the gods toward man, who is not wise and accordingly is not worthy of divine love. Diotima's conclusion is prepared by the earlier conversation between Socrates and Agathon, in which Agathon agrees that eros is desire, not of what we have, but of what we lack.[50] Thus, in Platonic terms our love for the gods cannot be requited.

Plotinus advances the example of the sage and his neighbour in 1.2 [19].5 to illustrate the relation between two different levels of the same soul. While the phases of the soul are the theme of this passage, we may examine what it says obliquely about Plotinus on the subject of human relationships. The sage next door does not pay any attention to us, at least in our capacity as aspiring sages. His improving effect on us arises simply from his being and abiding in what he is. He summons us to virtue: simply by being what he is, he offers a compelling model for our imitation.

In 1.2 [19].6, as we have seen, the relation of master and servant is similarly used to illustrate the relation of higher and lower soul. If again we thematize the human relationship, we obtain a similar result, as the thought of that passage extends the reasoning of the first. The notion of neighbourhood is again invoked as the master exercises his improving effect as a model for imitation upon the servant with whom he has taken up his dwelling (συνῳκίσθη).[51] We need not suppose any advertent act on the part of the master that would contribute to the servant's improvement in virtue.

Let us examine these relationships, as human relationships, in Platonic terms. The sage has wisdom and goodness and the man next door does not. As the sage does possess these qualities, he will not love his next door neighbour who lacks them, or at least, he cannot

49. 204a1–2.
50. 199e6–201a1.
51. 1.2 [19].6.9.

love these qualities in his neighbour if they are not to be found in him. As we have seen, Aristotle also entertains the prospect of this kind of autarchy on the part of the sage.

However, we need not say that the sage's neighbour derives no benefit from his neighbourhood. He is summoned by the virtue of the sage to the tasks of imitation and improvement. The neighbour may himself become a sage. If this happens, he will not indeed desire or love, but will possess the qualities of the sage. *Qua* good and virtuous, he will be at one with the sage and will share in his identity as sage.

The disciple's advertence is met with indifference by the sage. If we examine the relationship in phenomenological terms, we see that the sage's indifference is the complement of the disciple's advertence. The disciple admires the sage, his wisdom and his goodness. Wisdom and goodness are among the intentional objects that engage the attention of the disciple. Perhaps such items of awareness as facial expression, taste in art, etc., belong to the manifold of what the disciple experiences and finds attractive. As the disciple through imitation becomes more like his master, his attention to the inessential dissolves. Wisdom and virtue will remain as the object of focal awareness. The sage himself, as the substrate or vehicle of these inessential qualities, together with his characteristics and tastes, is relegated to the margin of awareness.

In the previous chapter[52] we discussed a passage in which Plotinus compares the progress towards the One of the soul to the person who enters the house of a great man.[53] At first he admires the furnishings and appointments of the house. As he notices the master of the house, the visitor focuses his attention upon him as an object worthy of an admiration well prepared by the magnificence of the house. As his vision blends with its object, what was formerly an object of vision (ὁρατόν) becomes vision itself (ὅρασις). The master is not just another thing to look at. We have entered into his way of looking at things which both produced the elegance of the house and is explicated by it.

It is the servant or disciple for whom the relation of master and servant or sage and disciple is thematic. The master has his mind on many things that lie outside the master/servant relationship: his ath-

52. p. 84.
53. 6.7 [38].35.7–16.

letic prowess, his social engagements, his civic work, his political re-
sponsibilities, his artistic or philosophical interests. The servant is
simply there, upon the margin of awareness, as a tool for certain tasks
embraced in the larger scheme of his commitments. However the
master may define his own identity, to the servant he is simply his
master and master alone. He is the focus of all identity.

Returning from this intersubjective relationship to the individual,
we see that the person who identifies himself contemplatively with the
highest principle in himself is the master of his servile passions. Such
a contemplative act may suspend engagement in the normal pursuit
of political advantage together with its temptations to corruption.
Paradoxically it is precisely this withdrawal from the common con-
cerns of political life that best fits him for public office because it
guarantees his integrity.[54]

In mitigation of Plotinus' account of mastership, it may be said that
he appears to prefer the (for ancient man) more liberal theory
that the master should rule by persuasion, rather than by force, and
that this persuasion may be exercised by the rhetorical *exemplum* of
his personality. Thus in a simile illustrating the relation between the
reasonable and passionate elements in the soul, the appearance of the
calm man (he manifests ἡσυχία) quiets the tumultuous crowd.[55]

We may find the example of the sage and his disciple more amenable
to our democratic tastes. It is the disciple or student for whom the
relationship of sage and disciple or teacher and student is thematic.
The teacher has his mind, not on pedagogy (unless he has had the
misfortune to attend a college of education), but upon his subject.
The student's attraction to a subject may well be mediated through
the teacher's personality, the reputation of the university, and many
other items of awareness. Years hence, the teacher may not even be
remembered. Yet the student will possess the subject that was always
for the teacher the *intentum*, e.g., an approach to Greek, or a way of
understanding philosophy.

---

54. 4.4 [28].17; cf. also 5.9 [5].1; 2.9 [33].9; and Prini, *Plotino e la genesi* 36–39.
Plotinus' preference for aristocratic regimes proceeds, at least in part, from his opposition to anarchic, egalitarian trends among contemporary Christian-Gnostics (2.9
[33].9).

55. 6.4 [22].15.23–32. We may compare Vergil *Aeneid* i.148–53 for the ruler who
tames the tumultuous crowd by the force of his personality; Xenophon *Oeconomicus*
xii.17–18 for the view that the good steward will inspire care in the servants only if he
is careful himself.

Often in our gaudy talk about relationships we confuse intensity with depth. An intense sexual relationship may leave little important residue behind it. Yet I might have had a teacher in elementary school, now long forgotten, who by her address to a subject and her very being gave me a priceless gift which outlived my memory of her person. In such a case, is the love of the student or disciple not requited? Is advertence on the part of the teacher a necessary requirement for love?

It is useful to consider the word that Porphyry uses when he says that Plotinus "was present" (συνῆν) at once to himself and to others.[56] The verb is *suneinai*. In the third chapter, we examined a semantic field or complex of vocabulary partly characterized by the occurrence of the prefix *sun-*, "with." We remarked that the ontological terms *sunousia* and *suneinai* and their cognitive equivalents *sunoran, sunaisthêsis, sunaisthanesthai, sunesis,* and *sunienai* offer an elastic vocabulary for the description of presence and dependence in the Plotinian universe.[57] These words (more easily than other words of presence that suggest an asymmetrical relation, such as *parousia*) may describe both a descending moment (of presence) and an ascending moment (of dependence or recognition of dependence that serves as the point of departure for ascent). The prefix itself, the notion of "withness," allows that elasticity.

The verb *suneinai* may describe, not only vertical presence or dependence, but presence to oneself. In the second chapter we discussed in some depth a text (5.4 [7].2) in which such presence to oneself is set forth.[58] There we saw that the presence of the One to itself is compared to the heat that is in the flame itself (as distinguished from the heat that is projected outward from the flame). The example of the flame and heat instantiates a general principle that, in the case of every essence, there are two acts, one inherent and intransitive, the other transitive and externally projected. The intransitive act of the One is described as "being with" the One (συνούσης ἐνεργείας).[59]

---

56. *Vita Plotini* 8.19.

57. The reader is referred to Schroeder, "*Synousia, Synaisthêsis* and *Synesis,*" for a full account of this vocabulary. Where in that study the focus was upon questions of presence and dependence, with some consideration of the erotic significance of these words, the emphasis here is upon their erotic aspect.

58. pp. 28–32.

59. 5.4 [7].2.35.

The presence of the One to itself is described at once in the language of eros and *sunousia*: "And he, that same self, is loveable and love and love of himself (αὐτοῦ ἔρως), in that he is beautiful only from himself and in himself. For surely his keeping company with himself (τὸ συνεῖναι ἑαυτῷ) could not be in any other way than if what keeps company and what it keeps company with were the one and the same" (6.8 [39].15.1–4). The phrase in Greek that describes the One's keeping company with itself (τὸ συνεῖναι ἑαυτῷ, 6.8 [39].15.3) is the same as that which Porphyry uses[60] to depict Plotinus' presence to himself (συνῆν ἑαυτῷ).

In this passage, the themes of presence and of love are brought together in a manner that defies the logic of Diotima, in Plato's Symposium, for whom none of the gods can love.[61] If love is love for that which we do not have, how can the One, the supreme god, be said to have love (eros) even of himself? This Plotinian transformation of eros may be understood from the use that he makes of the vocabulary of *sunousia*. We have seen that *sunousia* describes the relations of presence and dependence between (to observe Platonic language) Form and particular in such a way that this relationship becomes one of dynamic continuity. It embraces an elastic inventory of presence and dependence that includes, not only the presence of the source to the product, or the product to the source, but the presence of the source to itself. The entire circuit of presence and dependence is completed.

Sunousia is also used to describe the relationship of love. The noun *sunousia* and the verb *suneinai* are employed by Plato to describe human relationships: friendship or association;[62] the society of teacher and pupil;[63] heterosexual intercourse;[64] and homosexual love.[65] It also describes the union of the soul with Beauty.[66]

If we now construe *sunousia* not only as a term of metaphysics but also as a word properly belonging to the vocabulary of Platonic love, we shall see that our love for the One is also grounded in a radical withness within the One itself. Thus our love for the One does not

---

60. *Vita Plotini* 8.19.
61. 204a1–2.
62. *Protagoras* 347e1; *Symposium* 176e2.
63. *Gorgias* 515b2; *Politicus* 285c8.
64. *Symposium* 206c6.
65. *Symposium* 211d6 and 8.
66. *Symposium* 212a2.

depend upon our attempt to relate to the One, nor upon any attempt on the part of the One to relate to us. It is rather that, just as the One, simply by abiding in what it is, creates us, so it in that same abiding serves as the ground of all desire for itself.

Plotinus uses the word *sunousia* of human love[67] and also of love of the One (6.9 [9].9.44–45.): "There is the true object of eros, with whom we may be together (*suneinai*)." The word that Plotinus employs as the cognitive complement of *sunousia*, *sunaisthêsis*, is used by Aristotle in the *Nicomachean Ethics* to describe sharing the feelings or sentiments of a friend.[68] Plotinus says that the One:

– is contemplated in many beings, in each and every one of those capable of receiving him as another self (οἷον ἄλλον αὐτόν), just as the centre of a circle exists by itself, but every one of the radii in the circle has its point in the centre and their lines bring their individuality to it. For it is with something of this sort in ourselves that we are in contact with god and are with him (σύνεσμεν) and depend upon him; and those of us who converge towards him are firmly established in him. (5.1 [10].11.9–15)

With the words οἷον ἄλλον αὐτόν, "as another self", Plotinus refers to Aristotle's notion [69] that the friend is "another self" (ἄλλος αὐτός). The verb *suneinai* here describes how we are together with the One with the highest part of ourselves, just as the radius extends from the circumference of a circle to touch the centre. The verb here clearly expresses both ontic dependence and continuity, on the one hand, and friendship, on the other, i.e., both metaphysical and erotic senses. The word *sunaisthêsis*, which is used in Aristotle to express the sentiments of friendship, is not used in this passage but it certainly could have been. Perhaps the otherwise epistemological term *sunaisthêsis* bears the colour of love and friendship in Plotinus. It would then make an even more attractive complement to *sunousia* which carries this reference in addition to its ontological uses.

In 6.8 [39].15 the presence of the One to itself, as *sunousia*, and the notion that the One is love (eros) of itself are conjoined. In its metaphysical sense, *sunousia* may express the presence of the One to itself and its presence to its sequents. It may also express the de-

---

67. 1.6 [1].5.7; 6.7 [38].31.16.
68. *Nicomachean Ethics* ix.9.1170b10.
69. *Nicomachean Ethics* ix.9.1169b6–7; ix.9.1170b6–7.

pendence of the sequents upon the One. If we undertake an equation of the metaphysical and erotic senses of *sunousia*, it will make sense to say that if the One is present to itself, it may by that very fact be eros of itself. Such presence to self and love of self on the part of the One may be the foundation both of its presence to us and of its erotic relationship to us. It will also be the basis of our presence to and love of the One. Thus the circuit of eros is as self-connected and complete as is the circuit of presence and dependence.[70]

The hypostasis of Intellect is described as a transitive activity proceeding from the intransitive activity internal to the One, just as heat proceeds externally while heat remains within and consubstantial with the flame.[71] On this reasoning, we should expect there to be in the One (with no compromise of its unity) some principle that would correspond to Intellect, just as in the flame there is an internal heat that corresponds to the heat that proceeds externally from it. The inclusion of such a principle within the One would belong to the One's presence to itself, to its *sunousia*.

There is indeed a sense in which Intellect is itself prefigured in the One. Thus Intellect bears witness to a sort of Intellect in the One that is not Intellect (μαρτυρεῖν τὸν οἷον ἐν ἑνὶ νοῦν οὐ νοῦν ὄντα, 6.8 [39].18.21–22). This statement is a bold assertion of the principle stated at 5.3. [49].15.31–32 that the One possesses its attributes in such a way that they are not discrete (διακεκρίμενα), while in Intellect these same attributes are held in discrete form.[72] The Plotinian trinity of the One, Intellect, and Soul need not be regarded as the only expression of trinitarian thought in Plotinus. There are implicitly three moments in the relationship between the One and Intellect that form an important trinitarian relationship: the by now familiar moments of abiding, procession, and return. These moments also occur in the relationship between the Soul and Intellect.[73] Indeed this trin-

---

70. Cf. Bussanich, "Plotinus on the Inner Life of the One," 183: "Within the absolute itself must lie the prefiguration both of procession and return, which ultimately are mirror images of each other. The One must 'move into its interior' [the reference is to 6.8 [39].16.12–13] and 'be in love with itself' so that everything can come into existence and eventually return to the One."

71. 5.4 [7].2.26–33.

72. Cf. Schroeder, "The Platonic *Parmenides*," 68.

73. The One abides in the generation of Intellect which proceeds from itself (5.4 [7].2.19–22); the Intellect returns to its source in the One in an act of introspection (6.9 [9].2.35–36); the Soul likewise proceeds from Intellect while the Intellect abides

itarian relationship may is more important for the subsequent history of Christian trinitarian theology than the series of the three Plotinian hypostases, the One, Intellect, and Soul.[74]

Whether we look to the trinitarian series of the Plotinian hypostases or to the three moments in the relationship between the One and Intellect, we are in the presence of a subordinationist trinity. When we look to the prefiguration of Intellect in the One itself and the expression of that relationship in terms of the *sunousia* (witness as between flame and heat) internal to the One, may we not see a sort of trinity within the One itself? This trinity would consist of the One, the prefiguration of Intellect, and the relationship (*sunousia*) that exists between them.

Porphyry, we recall, described Plotinus' presence to himself and to others in terms of *sunousia*.[75] We have already seen how, in the case of intersubjective relationships, presence to oneself could entail presence to others. In that discussion we were not specifically addressing the lexicography of *sunousia*. We should, however, expect that *sunousia* on the part of the One would express presence to others, as well as presence to himself. For the One is said to be with all things (πᾶσι σύνεστιν).[76] As we have seen, *sunousia* as presence to oneself, presence to others, and dependence forms a complete circuit of dynamic continuity. Thus the presence of the One to others is an explication of its presence to itself, a co-presence that foreshadows Intellect as the second hypostasis. The horizontal *sunousia* or witness within the One must be the ultimate ground of our conversion toward and love of

---

what it is (5.2 [11].1.16–17); similarly, the Soul returns to Intellect (4.4 [28].2.25–27). We do not in Plotinus have the formal trinity μονή – πρόοδος – ἐπιστροφή as in Proclus (cf. Beierwaltes, *Denken des Einen*, 118–64). Nevertheless, the essential elements of this triad are to be found in Plotinus, cf. Beierwaltes, *Proklos*, 160; 162; Beierwaltes, "Neoplatonica," 132; Beierwaltes, *Platonismus und Idealismus*, 129–30.

74. For a thorough discussion of this topic see Beierwaltes, *Denken des Einen* and my review of this book, "Review of Beierwaltes, *Denken des Einen*." The discussion of a Plotinian background for the doctrine of the trinity has principally been discussed with reference to the sources of trinitarian doctrine in Marius Victorinus. For a history of this discussion, see Hadot, *Porphyre et Victorinus*, 1–30; the immediate source of Marius Victorinus is Porphyry's commentary on the Platonic *Parmenides* (cf. Hadot, *Porphyre et Victorinus*; Beierwaltes, *Identität und Differenz*, 57–74).

75. *Vita Plotini* 8.19

76. 6.9 [9].7.29.

the One since it prefigures the whole drama of procession and conversion.

Projecting this interpretation onto our understanding of the Platonic Form in Plotinus, we remind ourselves that the Form is of intrinsic value, quite apart from its relation to us or to the world. We may now add that it contains its relationship to us and our relationship to it *internally*. It contains our iconic attributes in the manner appropriate to an original or pattern and also contains within itself the relationships of "withness" and love in all their dimensions, so that these may unfold in the moments of abiding, procession, and conversion. There could be no more radical elimination of the Demiurge considered as an external agent of creation from the thought of Plotinus.

It was shown earlier that the beloved need not exert any advertent attention to improve the lover. The sage need not do anything but abide in what he is to confer his priceless gift of wisdom on his admiring pupils and neighbours. The same principle holds *a fortiori* with respect to our love for the divine. The response, while real, contains no advertence.

Paradoxically, our love is requited, but our beloved need not be aware of its return. Is there then no awareness of the lover on the part of the beloved? Can we truly feel requited love in the shadow of such oblivion? Perhaps we are not utterly abandoned by the erotic sentience of our beloved. Some awareness of products on the part of the source is indicated by Plotinus. He says of *natura artifex*: "in its own rest and as it were, awareness of itself (ἐν τῇ στάσει καὶ συναισθήσει), as in this awareness and consciousness (τῇ συνέσει ταύτῃ καὶ συναισθήσει) it saw the products which follow after it in a mode appropriate to it" (3.8 [30].4.18–20). Here the words *sunaisthêsis* and *sunesis* express a kind of awareness on the part of Nature and her sequents.

Sunaisthêsis is also used to describe consciousness of sequents on the part of the world soul[77] and awareness of sense impressions on the part of discursive reason.[78] Let us, however, speculate whether this could be extended beyond these instances. Let us suppose that *sunaisthêsis*, etc., form the necessary cognitive complement of *sunousia*.

---

77. 3.4 [15].4.10–11, and Smith, "Unconsciousness and Quasiconsciousness," 297–98.

78. 1.1 [53].9.20 and Smith *"Unconsciousness and Quasiconsciousness,"* 300 note 14.

Then *sunaisthêsis*, etc., would provide the epistemological equivalent of the elastic ontological inventory furnished by *sunousia*. We have seen that presence (*sunousia*) to oneself does not exclude, but rather extends to presence (*sunousia*) to others. If we take *sunaisthêsis* and *sunesis* as cognitive aspects of *sunousia*,[79] then the cognitive aspect of presence to self would likewise entail an extension of this cognitive aspect of presence to others. This need not mean that a superior principle would be conscious of its sequents. The aspect of awareness that complements its *sunousia*, its presence to itself and others, could also be presence to itself and others, in some manner.

Would this make any sense? Schwyzer properly notices[80] the trance-like character of the awareness expressed in 3.8 [30].4. Let us project this kind of subliminal awareness onto the Plotinian model of the sage and his disciple. The *intentum* of the sage's consciousness is his virtue. If he is a teacher, then it is his subject. The sage is not oblivious of his disciples, but they are relegated to the margin of awareness. We saw in the fourth chapter that, by the same token, soul in its ascent may yet retain passive memories of this world. If awareness is understood in this way, then we might be seen – as it were obliquely – at the margin of divine consciousness, yet within the halo of awareness. Yet we must be careful in this and remember that Plotinus is unclear as to whether we may attribute *sunaisthêsis* as self-consciousness to the One.[81]

The delicate question of advertence may be approached from a consideration of conversion in Plotinus. Aubin, in an extensive study of *epistrophê* or conversion (and the corresponding verb *epistrephein*), argues that in Plato and the ensuing extra-Christian tradition, including Plotinus, this word describes the turning of humanity toward God, but never describes divine advertence toward humanity.[82] By contrast, this word is employed in the Septuagint, the New Testament, and the Fathers as a word that may describe, as well as our address

---

79. Cf. pp. 51–52 above.

80. Schwyzer, "'Bewusst' und 'Unbewusst,'" 371–72.

81. Cf. 5.3 [49].13.13 and 21; 5.4 [7].2.18 and Schroeder "*Synousia, Synaisthêsis* and *Synesis*," 691–92; Gurtler, *Experience of Unity*, 49–84 argues cogently that *sunaisthêsis* contains two meanings: (1) fusion of a multitude of sensations; (2) self-awareness. In those texts in which *sunaisthêsis* is specifically denied to the One, it is the first and not the second sense which is in question. The first sense would, of course, compromise the unity of the One.

82. Aubin, *Problème de la "Conversion."*

to God, God's turning toward ourselves. However, there is a use of the verb *epistrephein* describing how Beauty turns us toward itself, even if it does not turn toward us. In the first chapter of his earliest work, *On Beauty*, Plotinus asks, "What is it that stirs the gaze of the beholders and turns them toward itself (ἐπιστρέφει πρὸς αὐτό) and compels them and causes them to rejoice in the vision?" (1.6 [1].1.17–19). It is that Beauty itself which crowns the ladder of love in Plato's *Symposium*.[83] Beauty, in its very abiding, summons us and turns us towards itself. Those who have properly approached the question of love in Plotinus have understood this subtle paradox.

By way of recapitulation, let us see how the present examination of love is grounded in those principles of interpretation that we have developed in previous chapters. We have seen that for Plotinus the Platonic Form is an intrinsically valuable object of intellective or spiritual vision, quite apart from its uses in ontological or epistemological explanation. As such it belongs rather to enjoyment than to use.

By extension, the particular is also to be enjoyed as it is in itself, free of entanglement in the web of providential relationships. The ox has horns, not for defence, but in order to be an ox. A true appreciation or enjoyment of the particular will exclude discursive comparison, on the scheme of representation, between the particular as image or copy and the Form as original or pattern.

Viewing the particular only from the horizon of its relationship to the Form precludes its enjoyment, just as seeing the Form only from the horizon of its relationship with the particular precludes true vision and enjoyment with respect to the Form. We can suspend our question about the relationship between the Form and the particular and open our reflection to the self-manifestation of the particular in its intrinsic value. Then we may truly enjoy the particular and in it find, in a deepening of that experience, a window through which we may both see and enjoy the Form that is its ground.

In the third chapter, we examined *sunousia* in the context of the presence of the intelligible world to us and our dependence upon it. We discovered that the "withness" expressed by that vocabulary functions in three distinct but closely related senses. It describes the presence of the source to us. Yet that presence is grounded in withness

---

83. Cf. 1.6 [1].1.20 and Plato *Symposium* 211c3; 1.6 [1].7.8–11 and Plato *Symposium* 211e1.

in the sense that expresses the unity and integrity of the source, even as the internal bond between the flame and heat is the ground of the outward projection of the heat from the flame. Similarly that witness that is located in the source itself is also the ground of our dependence upon, continuity with, and return to the source.

We also saw, in the third chapter, that the ontological witness of *sunousia* is complemented by an epistemological witness expressed by other words sharing the same prefix: *sunoran, sunaisthêsis* (and *sunaisthanesthai*) and *sunesis* (and *sunienai*). The light is "seen with" the things that it illumines, at first as an intentional object of marginal consciousness and then as an object of focal awareness to which we attend. As we deepen our awareness of light, we return from the externally directed witness of light projected outside the source (although always in dynamic continuity with it) to that witness or unity in which light and source of light are indistinguishable.

That all witness is grounded in the witness that is the unity and integrity of the source suggests that we shall not understand *sunousia* if we first approach it from the horizon of relationship. We must rather understand that *sunousia* is primarily located in the source itself and that that witness is the ground of our ability to stand in relationship to the source at all.

When we address the subject of love, we quite naturally wish to examine it as a relationship. For Plotinus love does indeed have much to do with witness. We have seen, however, that our presence to others is most deeply founded in our presence to ourselves. Further, the presence of the sage to himself is discovered to be a condition of dependence upon the One and the One's radical unity and identity turn out to be the perfect expression of presence to self. In identifying presence to self as the most fundamental source of our gifts to others, Plotinus avoids the mistake of confusing intensity with depth, a busy advertence with the contemplative gift of oneself. The final *intentum* of the sage's contemplation is the One, viewed in its intrinsic value and not sought for any purpose to do with its relationship to the world, either as explanation or as source of benefits to himself.

Yet the quest for the One is not an adventure undertaken by the individual alone. If Plotinus' presence to himself embraces a presence to others, then that presence need not be confined to exerting its influence on the individual. That presence can also be the foundation of community, a community founded not only in the dynamic presence of Plotinus but in the One itself. The meetings of Plotinus' circle are described by Porphyry as *sunousiai*.[84] In the fourth chapter, we had occasion to describe the hermeneutical circle of intuition and speech as the ground of activity in Plotinus' seminar. Of the address to the One, Plotinus says: "We speak and write impelling towards it."[85] We may see in this dimension of *sunousia* that for Plotinus and his circle philosophy was a living tradition and way of life, the pursuit of the One, the transcendent object addressed now by speech and now by intuition, the ground of their being together.[86] As we have seen, that meeting of minds and spirits is grounded and foreshadowed in the intrinsic nature of the One itself, properly described as "loveable and love and love of himself in that he is beautiful only from himself and in himself. For surely his keeping company with himself could not be in any other way than if what keeps company and what it keeps company with were the one and the same."[87]

---

84. *Vita Plotini* 1.13,14; 3.46; 5.6; 13.1; 14.10,21; 16.10; συνεῖναι τινι is used of the relationship of master and pupil, 7.2,12; 23.17; disciples are described as οἱ συνόντες, 3.37; cf. 4.8–9; 5.1 for συγγίγνεσθαι (another word with the συν- prefix) to describe this assocation, cf. Goulet-Cazé, "L'Arrière-plan scolaire," 232; 236 note 3 on Porphyry's vocabulary for this subject.

85. 6.9 [9].4.12–13.

86. On this communal aspect of Plotinus' school, see Beierwaltes, *Denken des Einen*, 110–13. For a study of the evidence of Porphyry's *Life of Plotinus* for the Plotinian community as a spiritual as well as a philosophical circle, see Goulet-Cazé, "L'Arrière-plan scolaire" 250; 254–57; 325–27; Hadot, "Neoplatonist Spirituality," 230–33; Hadot "Neoplatonist Spirituality," 232 remarks: "In fact, philosophizing, in a general way, in all the ancient schools is philosophizing together (*symphilosopheuein*) (Diogenes Laertius *Lives* 5.52; 10.18)." (The first of these reference to Diogenes Laertius should read "5.53").

87. 6.8 [39].15.1.1–4.

Bibliography

Angelus Silesius, *Sämtliche Poetische Werke*, ed. H. L. Held. 3 volumes. Munich: Carl Hansen, 1949.

Arnim, H. F. A. von (ed.), *Stoicorum Verterum Fragmenta*. 4 vols. Leipzig: Teubner, 1903–24. [Referred to as SVF].

Anton, J. P. "Plotinus' Refutation of Beauty as Symmetry." *Journal of Aesthetics and Art Criticism* 23 (1964): 233–37.

Armstrong, A. H. (trans.) *Plotinus*. 7 vols. London and Cambridge, Mass.: Heinemann 1966–88 [referred to as "Armstrong"].

— "Plotinus." In *Cambridge History of Later Greek and Medieval Philosophy*, edited by A. H. Armstrong, Part 3, 195–263. Cambridge: Cambridge University Press, 1967.

— "Neoplatonic Valuation of Nature, Body and Intellect." *Augustinian Studies* 3 (1972): 35–49.

— "Tradition, Reason and Experience in the Thought of Plotinus." In *Plotino e il Neoplatonismo in Oriente e in Occidente*, 171–194 Rome: Accademia Nazionale dei Lincei, 1974.

— "Beauty and the Discovery of Divinity in the Thought of Plotinus." In *Kephalaion. Studies in Greek Philosophy and its Continuation presented to Professor C. J. De Vogel*, edited by J. M. Mansfeld and L.M. de Rijk, 155–63 Assen: Van Gorcum, 1975.

— "Form, Individual and Person in Plotinus." *Dionysius* 1 (1977): 49–68.

Arnou, R. *Le Désir de Dieu dans la Philosophie de Plotin*. Rome: Presses de l'Université Grégorienne, 1967.

Aubin, P. "L' image dans l'oeuvre de Plotin." *Recherches de Sciences Religieuses* 41 (1953): 348–79.

— *Le Problème de la "Conversion". Étude sur un terme commun a l'hellénisme et au christianisme des trois premiers siècles*. Paris: Beauchesne, 1963.

Barbanti, M. di P. *La metafora in Plotino*. Catania: Bonano Editore, 1981.

Beierwaltes, W. "Plotins Metaphysik des Lichtes." *Zeitschrift für Philosophische Forschung* 15 (1961): 334–62; reprinted in *Die Philosophie des Neuplatonismus*, edited by C. Zintzen, 75–115 *Wege der Forschung* 186. Darmstadt: Wissenschaftliche Buchgesellschaft, 1971.

– *Proklos. Grundzüge seiner Metaphysik*. Frankfurt: Klostermann, 1965.

– *Plotin. Über Ewigkeit und Zeit* (*Komm. zu Enneade III* 7). Frankfurt: Klostermann, 1967.

– "Neoplatonica." *Philosophische Rundschau* 16 (1969): 130–52.

– *Nachwort* to "Plotins Metaphysik des Lichtes" (see above) in the reprint of that article in *Die Philosophie des Neuplatonismus*, edited by C. Zintzen, 116–17 *Wege der Forschung* 186 Darmstadt: Wissenschaftliche Buchgesellschaft, 1971.

– *Platonismus und Idealismus*. Frankfurt am Main: Klostermann, 1972.

– *Identität und Differenz*. Frankfurt am Main: Klostermann, 1980.

– "Image and Counterimage? Reflections on Neoplatonic Thought with respect to its place to-day." In *Neoplatonism and Early Christian Thought. Essays in honour of A. H. Armstrong*, edited by H. J. Blumenthal and R. A. Markus, 236–45. Variorum: London, 1981.

– *Denken des Einen. Studien zur Neuplatonischen Philosophie und ihrer Wirkungsgeschichte*. Frankfurt am Main: Klostermann, 1985.

Blumenthal, H.J. *Plotinus' Psychology, his Doctrines of the Embodied Soul*. The Hague: Martinus Nijhoff, 1971.

– "Plotinus in the Light of Twenty Years' Scholarship, 1951–1971." In *Aufstieg und Niedergang der Römischen Welt*, 2.36.1, edited by W. Haase, 528–70, Berlin and New York: de Gruyter, 1987.

Bréhier, E. *La philosophie de Plotin*. Paris: Boivin, 1928.

Buchner, H. *Plotins Möglichkeitslehre*. Munich and Salzburg: A.Pustet, 1970.

Bussanich, J. "Plotinus on the Inner Life of the One." *Ancient Philosophy* 7 (1987): 163–89.

Charles-Saget, A. *L'Architecture du Divin. Mathématique et Philosophie chez Plotin et Proclus*. Paris: Les Belles Lettres, 1982.

Charrue, J.-M. *Plotin Lecteur de Platon*. Paris: Les Belles Lettres, 1978.

Cilento, V. "Stile e linguaggio nella filosofia di Plotino." *Vichiana* 4 (1967): 29–41.

– "Stile, Linguaggio, Poesia." In *Saggi su Plotino*. Milan: U. Mursia, 1973, 201–39.

Corrigan, K. and O'Cleirigh, P. "The Course of Plotinian Scholarship from 1961 to 1986." *Aufstieg und Niedergang der Römischen Welt*, 2.36.1, edited by W. Haase, 571–623. Berlin and New York: de Gruyter, 1987.

Crome, P. *Symbol und Unzulänglichkeit der Sprache.* Munich: W. Fink, 1970.

de Keyser, E. *La Signification de l'art dans les Ennéades de Plotin.* Louvain: Bibliothèque de l'Université, 1955.

Dodds, E. R. "Tradition and Personal Achievement in the Philosophy of Plotinus," *Journal of Roman Studies* 50 (1960): 1–7; reprinted in: E. R. Dodds, *The Ancient Concept of Progress,* 126–39, Oxford: Oxford at the Clarendon Press, 1973.

Dörrie, H. "Emanation: Ein unphilosophisches Wort im spätantiken Denken." In *Parusia, Studien zur Philosophie Platons und zur Problemgeschichte des Platonismus. Festgabe für Johannes Hirschberger,* 119–41 (Frankfurt am Main: Minerva, 1965); reprinted in *idem Platonica Minora. Studia et testimonia antiqua 8,* 70–88, Munich: Wilhelm Fink, 1976.

Fazzo, V. *La giustificazione delle immagini religiose dalla tarda antichità al Cristianesimo.* Naples: Nuova Collana Saggi Napoli. Ed. scientif. ital., 1977.

Ferwerda, R. *La signification des images et des métaphores dans la pensée de Plotin.* Groningen: J. B. Wolters, 1965.

Fielder, J. "Plotinus' Copy Theory." *Apeiron* 11, no. 2 (1977): 1–16.

– "Plotinus' Reply to the Arguments of *Parmenides* 130a–131d." *Apeiron* 12, no. 2 (1978): 1–5.

– "A Plotinian View of Self-Predication and TMA." *Modern Schoolman* 57 (1980): 339–47.

Frutiger, P., *Les mythes de Platon. Étude philosophique et littéraire.* Paris: F. Alcan, 1930.

Gandillac, M. de "Plotin et la Métaphysique d'Aristote." In *Études sur la Métaphysique d'Aristote. Actes du VIe Symposium Aristotelicum,* edited by P. Aubenque, 247–59 (and the "Discussion" 260–64), Paris: Vrin, 1979, 247–59.

Goulet-Cazé, M.-O. "L'Arrière-plan scolaire de la *Vie de Plotin.*" *Porphyre, La Vie de Plotin,* vol. 1, edited by L. Brisson, M.-O. Goulet-Cazé, R. Goulet and D. O'Brien, 229–327. Paris: Vrin, 1982.

Grabar, A. "Plotin et les origines de l'esthétique médiévale," *L'art de la fin de l'antiquité et du moyen âge.* 3 vols., 1: 15–29, Paris: Collège de France, 1968.

Gurtler, G. M. "Human Consciousness and its Intersubjective Dimension in Plotinus." Ph.D. dissertation, Fordham University, 1978.

– *Plotinus. The Experience of Unity.* New York: Peter Lange, 1988.

Hadot, P. *Plotin ou la simplicité du regard.* Paris: Plon, 1963.

– *Porphyre et Victorinus.* Paris: Études Augustiniennes, 1968.

– "Philosophie, Dialectique, Rhétorique dans l'antiquité." *Studia Philosophica* 39 (1980): 139–66.

– "Ouranos, Kronos, and Zeus in Plotinus' Treatise against the Gnostics." In *Neoplatonism and Early Christian Thought. Essays in Honour of A. H. Armstrong,* edited by H. J. Blumenthal and R. A. Markus, 124–37. London: Variorum, 1981.

– *Exercices Spirituels et Philosophie Antique*. Paris: Études Augustiennes, 1981.

– "Neoplatonist Spirituality. I. Plotinus and Porphyry." *Classical Mediterranean Spirituality. Egyptian Greek Roman. World Spirituality* 15, edited by A. H. Armstrong, 230–49. New York: Crossroads, 1986.

– "Structure et Thèmes du traité 38 de Plotin." *Aufstieg und Niedergang der Römischen Welt* 2.36.1, ed. W. Haase, 625–76, Berlin and New York, 1987.

Harder, R., continued by R. Beutler and W. Theiler . *Plotins Schriften*. 5 vols. Hamburg: Felix Meiner, 1956–60. [Translation and commentary referred to as "HBT"].

Heidegger, M. *Der Satz vom Grund*. Pfullingen: Günther Neske, 1957.

– *Die Grundprobleme der Phänomenologie*. Frankfurt am Main: Friedrich-Willhelm von Herrmann, 1975.

Helleman-Elgersma, W. *Soul-Sisters. A Commentary on Enneads IV.3 [27].1–8*. Ph.D. dissertation, Free University of Amsterdam, 1980.

Henry, P. "Une comparaison chez Aristote, Alexandre et Plotin." In *Les Sources de Plotin*, edited by E. R. Dodds, *Entretiens sur l'Antiquité classique* 5, 427–44 and the "Discussion," 445–49. Fondation Hardt: Vandoeuvres and Geneva, 1957.

Henry, P. and Schwyzer, H.-R. *Plotini Opera*. 3 vols. Oxford: Oxford University Press, 1964–1982, the *editio minor* [referred to as "H-S"].

Husserl, E. *Ideen zu einer reinen Phänomenologie und Phänomenologischen Philosophie*, Book I, *Allgemeine Einführung in die reine Phänomenologie*, edited by Karl Schuhmann. The Hague: Martinus Nijhoff, 1976.

Lewy, H. *Chaldaean Oracles and Theurgy*. Cairo: Publications de l'Institut français d'archéologie orientale, 1956.

Lloyd, A. C. "Non-discursive thought – An Enigma of Greek Philosophy." *Proceedings of the Aristotelian Society*, n.s. 70 (1969–70): 261–74.

MacKenna, Stephen (trans.) *Plotinus, The Enneads*, third edition revised by B. S. Page. London: Faber and Faber, 1962 [referred to as "MacKenna"].

Matter, P. P. *Zum Einfluss des Platonischen "Timaeus" auf das Denken Plotins*. Winterthur: Keller, 1964.

Miller, C. L. "Union with the One, Ennead 6,9,8–11." *The New Scholasticism* 51 (1977): 182–95.

O'Daly, G. J. P. *Plotinus' Philosophy of Self*. Shannon: Irish University Press, 1973.

– "Memory in Plotinus and two Early Texts of St. Augustine." *Studia Patristica* 14, edited by E. Livingstone, 461–69, Berlin: Akademie-Verlag, 1976.

O'Meara, D. J. "A propos d'un témoignage sur l'expérience mystique chez Plotin." *Mnemosyne* 27, series 4 (1974): 238–44.

Pelikan, J. *The Light of the World. A Basic Image in Early Christian Thought.* New York: Harper, 1962.

Pépin, J. *Mythe et Allégorie.* Paris: Éditions Montaigne, 1958; reprint Paris: Études Augustiniennes, 1977.

– "Héraklès et son Reflet." In *Le Néoplatonisme, Colloques Internationaux du Centre National de las Recherche Scientifique, Sciences humaines, Royaumont 9–13 June 1969*, edited by M. G. Laizeau and M. A. Segonds, 167–92. Paris: Éditions du centre national de la recherche scientifique, 1971.

Perler, O. *Der Nus bei Plotin und das Verbum bei Augustinus als vorbildliche Ursache der Welt.* Freiburg, Sw.: Studia Friburgensia, 1931.

Phillips, J. F. "The Universe as Prophet. A Soteriological Formula in Plotinus." *Greek, Roman and Byzantine Studies* 22 (1981): 269–81.

Plass, P. "Plotinus' Ethical Theory." *Illinois Classical Studies* 7 (1982): 241–59.

Prini, P. *Plotino e la genesi dell' umanesimo interiore.* Rome: Ed. Abete, 1968.

Rich, A. N. M. "Reincarnation in Plotinus." *Mnemosyne*, series 4, no. 10 (1957): 232–38.

– "Plotinus and the theory of artistic imitation." *Mnemosyne*, series 4, no. 13 (1960): 233–39.

Rist, J. M. "Mysticism and Transcendence in Later Neoplatonism." *Hermes* 92 (1964): 213–25.

– *Plotinus. The Road to Reality.* Cambridge: Cambridge University Press, 1967.

Robinson, T. M., *Plato's Psychology.* Toronto: University of Toronto Press, 1970.

Schroeder, F. M. "The Platonic *Parmenides* and Imitation in Plotinus." *Dionysius* 2 (1978): 51–73.

– "Representation and Reflection in Plotinus." *Dionysius* 4 (1980): 37–59.

– "The Analogy of the Active Intellect to Light in the 'De Anima' of Alexander of Aphrodisias." *Hermes* 109 (1981): 215–25.

– "Light and the Active Intellect in Alexander and Plotinus." *Hermes* 112 (1984): 239–48.

– "Saying and Having in Plotinus," *Dionysius* 9 (1985): 75–84.

– "Conversion and Consciousness in Plotinus, *Enneads* 5.1 [10].7." *Hermes* 114 (1986): 186–96.

– "The Self in Ancient Religious Experience." *Classical Mediterranean Spirituality. Egyptian Greek Roman. World Spirituality* 15, edited by A. H. Armstrong, 336–59. New York: Crossroads 1986.

– "Ammonius Saccas." *Aufstieg und Niedergang der Römischen Welt*, 2.36.1, edited by W. Haase, 493–526, Berlin and New York: de Gruyter, 1987.

– "*Synousia, Synaisthêsis* and *Synesis*: Presence and Dependence in the Plotinian Philosophy of Consciousness." *Aufstieg und Niedergang der Römischen Welt*, 2.36.1, edited by W. Haase, 677–99. Berlin: de Gruyter, 1987.

– Review of Werner Beierwaltes, *Denken des Einen. Studien zur Neuplatonischen Philosophie und ihrer Wirkungsgeschichte.* Frankfurt-am-Main: Klostermann, 1985. In *Philosophisches Jahrbuch der Görres-Gesellschaft* 95.1 (1988): 195–98.

Schroeder, F. M. and Todd, R. B. *Two Greek Aristotelian Commentators on the Intellect.* The *De Intellectu* Attributed to Alexander of Aphrodisias and Themistius' Paraphrase of Aristotle *De Anima* 3.4–8. Introduction, Translation, Commentary and Notes. Toronto: Pontifical Institute of Mediaeval Studies, 1990.

Schwyzer, H.-R. "Plotinus." In *Paulys Real-Encylopädie der classischen Altertumswissenschaft,* vol. 21, edited by K. Ziegler, cols. 471–592. Waldsee: Druckenmüller, 1951.

– "'Bewusst' und 'Unbewusst' bei Plotin." In *Les Sources de Plotin,* edited by E.R. Dodds, *Entretiens sur l'Antiquité Classique,* vol. 5, 341–79, Vandoeuvres-Geneva: Fondation Hardt, 1960.

Seidl, H. "L'union mystique dans l'explication de Plotin." *Revue Thomiste* 85 (1985): 253–64.

Shapiro, H. A. "*Heros Theos*: The Death and Apotheosis of Herakles." *Classical World* 77 (1983): 7–18.

Sinnige, T. G. "Metaphysical and Personal Religion in Plotinus." In *Kephalaion. Studies in Greek Philosophy offered to Professor C. J. De Vogel,* edited by J. M. Mansfeld and L. M. de Rijk, 147–54. Assen: Van Gorcum, 1975.

– "Gnostic influences in the early works of Plotinus and in Augustine." In *Plotinus amid Gnostics and Christians,* edited by D. T. Runia, 73–97. Amsterdam: Free University Press, 1984.

Sleeman, J. H. and Pollet, G. *Lexicon Plotinianum.* Leiden and Louvain: E. J. Brill, Leiden and Leuven University Press, 1980. [Referred to as "Sleeman and Pollet"].

Smith, A. "Unconsciousness and Quasiconsciousness in Plotinus." *Phronesis* 23 (1978): 292–301.

Sorabji, R. "Myths about non-propositional thought." In *Language and Logos, Studies in ancient Greek philosophy presented to G. E. L. Owen,* edited by M. Schofield and M. C. Nussbaum, 295–314. Cambridge: Cambridge University Press, 1982.

Theiler, W. "Die Sprache des Geistes in der Antike." *Forschungen zum Neuplatonismus,* 302–12. Berlin: de Gruyter, 1966.

Trouillard, J. "The Logic of Attribution in Plotinus." *International Philosophical Quarterly* 1 (1961): 125–38.

– "Valeur critique de la mystique plotinienne." *Revue Philosophique de Louvain* 59 (1961): 431–44.

Wilamowitz, U. von *Euripides Herakles.* 2 vols. Berlin: Weidmannsche Buchhandlung, 1895.

Index Locorum

References are to the text of Plotinus, as edited by Porphyry.

1.1 [53].8: 84; 1.1 [53].9: 109n78; 1.1
[53].12: 86;
1.2 [19].1: 93n11, 95n18, 97n24; 1.2
[19].2: 12n31, 97n25; 1.2 [19].4:
51n40; 1.2 [19].5: 92n5, 95, 95n19,
96, 96n20, 99n37, 101; 1.2 [19].6: 92,
92n6, 93–94, 95, 96, 97, 97n28,
98n29, 99n37, 101, 101n51; 1.2
[19].7: 97, 97n25;
1.4 [46].9: 82n60; 1.4 [46].10: 7n20,
54n50, 55n53, 58n63, 60n66, 61n67,
80n50, 82n59; 1.4 [46].15: 92n7,
97n27;
1.6 [1].1: 7n19, 20n50, 20n52, 21n54,
59n65, 72n21, 111, 111n83; 1.6 [1].2:
20n52, 52n42; 1.6 [1].3, 3; 1.6 [1].5:
106n67; 1.6 [1].7: 46, 47, 80n50,
111n83; 1.6 [1].8: 47, 84n69; 1.6
[1].9, 9n24, 84n69, 91n4, 100n46;
1.7 [54].1: 43, 53n49

2.1 [40].8: 35n34;
2.4 [12].5: 22n61;
2.6 [17].1: 14; 2.6 [17].3: 14;
2.8 [35].1: 21n57;
2.9 [33].1: 82n60; 2.9 [33].4: 36n38; 2.9
[33].9: 103n54; 2.9 [33].16: 7, 12n30,
56n59

3.1 [3].8: 19;
3.2 [47].2: 44; 3.2 [47].3: 72–73; 3.2
[47].13: 82n57; 3.2 [47].17: 21n54;
3.3 [48].6: 71;
3.4 [15].2: 82n57; 3.4 [15].4: 109n77;

3.5 [50].1: 52n42; 3.5 [50].9: 79n47;
3.7 [45].1: 12n29; 3.7 [45].6: 67;
3.8 [30].3: 45n13; 3.8 [30].4: 45n15, 65,
109, 110; 3.8 [30].5: 23n64; 3.8
[30].6: 76, 77n42; 3.8 [30].10: 32n26,
45n18; 3.8 [10].11: 41n4

4.3 [27].1: 66n2; 4.3 [27].5: 84n64; 4.3
[27].6: 10; 4.3 [27].10: 57n62; 4.3
[27].11: 57; 4.3 [27].17: 28n13; 4.3
[27].18: 57, 75n34, 88n87; 4.3
[27].25: 12n29; 4.3 [27].27: 86n77;
4.3 [27].30: 55n54; 4.3 [27].31:
88n88; 4.3 [27].32: 86n77, 86n78,
88n84;
4.4 [28].1: 86n78; 4.4 [28].2: 107n73;
4.4 [28].3: 87; 4.4 [28].4: 82n60,
87n80, 88; 4.4 [28].5: 12n29, 87,
88n85; 4.4 [28].17: 103n54;
4.5 [29]: 48n29; 4.5 [29].7: 3, 3n1, 26,
28, 28n10, 32, 33n29, 34n32, 35, 46,
50, 53, 61n67, 98n30;
4.6 [41].1: 22n59; 4.6 [41].2: 22n60; 4.6
[41].3: 15n37;
4.7 [2].6: 21n56; 4.7 [2].12: 12n29;
4.8 [6].1: 5, 5n6, 56; 4.8 [6].6: 8

5.1 [10].2: 64; 5. 1 [10].3: 35n34, 41,
42n7; 5. 1 [10].6: 32n25, 34, 41n3,
42, 47n27, 51n39; 5. 1 [10].7: 9, 42,
66n2; 5. 1 [10].8: 56n58, 81; 5. 1
[10].11: 106;
5.2 [11].1: 107n73;
5.3 [49].3: 83; 5.3 [49].4: 83, 84; 5.3

[49].8: 76; 5.3 [49].10: 75; 5.3
[49].13: 15n35,; 52n41, 75n33;
110n81; 5.3 [49].14: 67–70, 73,
78n46, 89; 110n81; 5.3 [49].15: 14,
30n19, 107; 5.3 [49].17: 85n72;
5.4 [7].2: 28–30, 31, 36n36, 51, 52n4,
107n71, 110n81;
5.5 [32].1: 16; 5.5 [32].6: 63n69; 5.5
[32].7: 32n28, 45n19, 48–49, 50, 52;
5.5 [32].8: 45–46; 46n21, 47, 50, 53,
62, 69n10, 85n71;
5.8 [31].1: 56n61, 57n62; 5.8 [31].3: 16;
5.8 [31].4: 15, 22, 60–61; 5.8 [31].5:
74n30, 76n38; 5.8 [31].6: 74n32,
76n39, 83; 5.8 [31].7: 36n38; 5.8
[31].10: 22n62; 5.8 [31].11: 23,
52n43; 5.8 [31].12: 36n38, 41n4,
42n8, 55n55;
5.9 [5].1: 103n54; 5.9 [5].5: 12n29; 5.9
[5].8: 16n40; 5.9 [5].9: 10

6.2 [9].4: 78, 90;
6.3 [44].15: 14;
6.4 [22]: 30; 6.4 [22].7: 9n24, 24n1,
32n28, 33n29; 6.4 [22].8: 32n27; 6.4
[22].9: 31, 31n20, 32, 50, 51; 6.4
[22].10: 31, 31n20, 32, 39; 6.4
[22].15: 103n55; 6.4 [22].16: 86n76;
6.5 [23]: 30; 6.5 [23].3: 53n46; 6.5

[23].7: 46n23; 6.5 [23].10: 89n92; 6.5
[23].12: 53n45;
6.7 [38].1: 17n44; 6.7 [38].2: 17, 71n15;
6.7 [38].3: 18, 71, 106n67; 6.7 [38].6:
7, 15, 82n57; 6.7 [38].7: 82n57; 6.7
[38].10: 18, 71n16; 6.7 [38].12: 7n20;
6.7 [38].15: 9; 6.7 [38].16: 52n42; 6.7
[38].17: 63n19, 73; 6.7 [38].22:
20n53, 72, 72n17, 73; 6.7 [38].23: 72,
73; 6.7 [38].24: 66n2; 6.7 [38].28:
63n69; 6.7 [38].29: 66n2; 6.7 [38].32:
63n69; 6.7 [38].33: 63n69; 6.7
[38].34: 87n82; 6.7 [38].35: 6, 69n10,
84n68, 102n53; 6.7 [38].36: 50n35;
6.7 [38].38: 67, 75n34; 6.7 [38].41:
52n41;
6.8 [39].7: 66n2; 6.8 [39].15: 105, 106,
113n87; 6.8 [39].16: 107n70; 6.8
[39].18: 107;
6.9 [9].2: 107n73; 6.9 [9].3: 52n43, 62,
64, 69, 85n70; 6.9 [9].4: 90, 113n85;
6.9 [9].5: 7n20; 6.9 [9].6: 81; 6.9
[9].7: 51n37, 51n38, 74, 75n35,
75n36, 79n48, 83n63, 108n76; 6.9
[9].8: 53n49, 89n89; 6.9 [9].9: 44,
47n26, 53n49, 63, 64n73, 80, 106; 6.9
[9].10: 53n49, 63, 80, 81n51; 6.9
[9].11: 62, 63n68, 84n67

General Index

Abiding, 28–30, 34, 34n33, 35, 36,
36n36, 41, 42n9, 43, 44, 45, 46–7, 54,
61, 63, 79, 80, 89, 94, 96, 97, 98, 99,
101, 106, 107, 109, 111; μένειν, 28,
29, 34, 36, 43, 44, 45, 46, 47, 97;
περιμένειν; μονή 3, 107n73
Alexander of Aphrodisias, 27, 28, 34
Ammonius Saccas, 5n6
ἀνάμνησις (anamnêsis). See Memory and
recollection
Angelus Silesius, 18n49
Anton J.P., 21n54
Aristophanes, 55n52, 94n13
Aristotle, 10, 17, 18n47, 26, 30, 34, 36,
41, 42, 84n65, 99, 100, 106
Armstrong, A.H., xi, 5, 5n5, 20n51,
21n58, 35n34, 45n15, 48n29, 69n11,
75n37, 80, 82n57
Arnim, H.F.A. von, xii, 20
Arnou, R., 47n26
Athanasius, 33n29
Aubin, P., 33n29, 110n82
Augustine, 20, 73, 73n25

Barbanti, M.di. P., 33n29
Begetting, 40–42, 42n9, 44, 64, 65
Beierwaltes, W., 33n29, 35n34, 68n8,
75n34, 77n41, 108n73, 113n86
Blumenthal, H., xi, 33n29, 55n54,
63n69
Bréhier, E., 7n20, 66n2
Buchner, H., 30n16
Bussanich, J., 107n70

Charles-Saget, A., 77n43
Charrue, J.-M., 33n29

Christ, 3
Cicero, 20n51
Cilento, V., 33, 66n2
Continuity. See Dynamic continuity
Conversion (ἐπιστροφή, ἐπιστρέφειν),
107n73; 110–11
"Copy-likeness" argument, 10–11, 13,
15
Corrigan, K., xi
Crantor, 36
Crome, P., 76n38

"Day and sail" argument, 8, 13, 15, 16,
24, 24n3, 32
de Keyser, E., 74n31, 76n40
Demiurge, demiurgic, 16–17, 17n44, 36,
38, 109
Diogenes Laertius, 113n86
Discussion, disclosure, declaration, 67–
80, 87, 89–90
Dodds, E.R., 92n8
Dörrie, H., 35n34
Dynamic continuity, 24, 25, 32, 39, 59–
60, 75–76, 92, 105, 108, 112

Emanation, 34–35

Fazzo, V., 57n62
Ferwerda, R., 33n29
Fielder, J., 9n24, 15n38, 16n39, 33n29
Frutiger, P., 36n37

Gandillac, M. De, 30n17
Gnosticism, 36n28, 103n54
Goulet-Cazé, M.-O., 66n2, 113n86
Grabar, A., 23 and n63

Grace, 72
Gurtler, G.M., 89n92, 110n81

Hadot, P., 7n20, 18n49, 36n38, 41n4, 63n69, 66n2, 70n14, 72, 72n18, 88n83, 91n2, 108n74, 113n86
Harder, R., Beutler, R., and Theiler, xii, 48n29, 67, 67n5
Having. *See* Saying and having
Hegel, G.W.F., 75n34
Heidegger, M., 18n49, 63n71
Helleman-Elgersma, W., 66n2
Henry, P., 21
Henry, P., and Schwyzer, H.-R., xii, 43n11, 45n15
Hesiod, 41n4
Homer, 46n22, 86n74
Husserl, E., 49n31

Illumination, 3–4, 9, 24–65 *passim*, 71, 72, 79. *See also* Reflection
Internal mirroring, 61. *See also* Reflection
Intrinsic value, 4, 6, 13, 15, 16, 18, 19, 23, 25, 36-39, 47, 49, 54, 71, 89–90, 111

Kronos, 41, 41n4, 42

Language, 66–90 *passim*, 113
Lewy, H., 72n24
Light. *See* Illumination
Lloyd, A.C., 75n34
Love, 4, 6–7, 11, 42, 46, 88, 91–113 *passim*

MacKenna, S., xii, 4n2, 5
"Mastership argument", 96–99
Matter, P.P., 17n46
Memory and recollection, 11–12, 56, 58–59, 81, 82, 86–88; *anamnêsis*, 11, 58, 81
Miller, C.L., 81n54

New Testament, 110

O'Cleirigh, P., xi
O'Daly, G.J.P., 12n29, 81n56, 88n88, 94n12
O'Meara, D.J., 5, 6n7
Openness. *See* Self-manifestation and openness

Optics 21–23
Ouranos, 41, 41n4

παρακολούθησις (*parakolouthêsis*), 82, 87
Pausanias, 47n26, 55n51
Pelikan, J., 33n29
Pépin, J., 41n4, 86n75
Perler, O., 73n25
Phillips, J.F., 73n26
Pindar, 86n79
Plass, J., 96n21
Plato, 3, 4, 6, 7, 9, 10, 11, 12, 15n38, 16, 17, 18n47, 29, 30, 32, 36, 41, 43, 43n10, 46, 47, 53, 55, 56, 56n58, 58, 60n66, 63, 67n4, 69, 70, 72, 73n29, 78, 81, 83n61, 84, 90, 91, 93, 95, 96, 97, 100, 101, 103, 111
Plutarch, 36n37, 55n52
Porphyry, xi-xii, 5n6, 27n7, 66, 91, 104, 105, 108n74, 113n84, 113n86
Presence and dependence, 8, 26–28, 41, 45–56, 91–113 *passim*
– real presence, 39, 55, 59–60, 76
– presence: παρεῖναι (*pareinai*), 26, 28, 41, 46, 53; παρουσία (*parousia*), 53, 104
– withness, 47–52, 61, 104–10, 112–13; συγγίγνεσθαι (*sungignesthai*), 113n84; συναισθάνεσθαι (*sunaisthanesthai*), 52n41, 52n42, 52n43, 104, 112; συναίσθησις (*sunaisthêsis*), 52n41, 52n42, 52n43, 104, 109, 110, 110n81, 112; συνεῖναι (*suneinai*), 50, 51, 91, 104, 105, 106, 107, 108, 113n84; σύνεσις (*sunesis*), 52, 52n41, 52n43, 104, 109, 110, 112; συνιέναι (*sunienai*), 52, 52n42, 104, 112; συνοικίζεσθαι (*sunoikizesthai*), 93, 101; συνορᾶν (*sunoran*), 48, 49, 50, 104, 112; συνουσία (*sunousia*), 53, 104, 109, 110, 112, 113
Prini, P., 103n54
Proclus, 36n37, 107n73
Pythagoreanism, 86n75

Reading, 76, 82–84; ἀνελίττω, 83, 84; ἐξελίττω, 84n64
Recollection. *See* Memory and recollection
Reflection, 3, 25–28, 37–39, 40–44, 49, 55–62, 75, 76; representation and, 37–39, 55–62, 75, 76; ἐμφαίνειν, 60; ἐνορᾶσθαι, 61. *See also* Illumination

Reincarnation, 82
Representation. *See* Reflection
Rich, A.N.M., 57n62, 82n57
Rist, J.M., 69n10, 89n91
Robinson, T.M., 36n37

Saying and having, 68–69, 77
Schroeder, F.M., 9n25, 12n30, 14n34,
   15n38, 24n3, 30n18, 32n34, 37n39,
   40n1, 52n41, 52n42, 52n43, 55n52,
   66n2, 76n38, 85n73, 86n78, 94n12
   94n15, 98n34, 98n35, 100n46,
   104n57, 107n72, 108n74, 110n81
Schroeder, F.M., and Todd, R.B., 28n11
Schwyzer, H.-R., 7n20, 110n80
Seidl, H., 81n54
Self, 85–90, 91–99; ταὐτότης, 95
Self-manifestation and openness, 19, 50,
   111
Semantic field, 43, 54, 104
Septuagint, 110
Shapiro, H.A., 86n79
Silence, 40–65 *passim*, 67, 77, 96, 103;
   ἡσυχία, 54, 77, 95, 103; ἡσύχως
   (*hêsuchôs*), 77; σιώπη, 43; σιωπᾶν, 45.
   See also Reflection
Sinnige, T.G., 36n38, 53n49
Sleeman, J.H., and Pollet, G., xii, 68n6

Smith, A., 109n77, 109n78
Sorabji, R. 75n34
Stobaeus, 20n51
Stoicism, 20, 20n51, 30n18
sunaisthêsis, sunesis, sunousia. *See* Presence
   and dependence, withness
Symmetry of predication, 62

Theiler, W., 75n34, 88n87
Theocritus, 94n13
Theophrastus, 94n13
"Third man" argument, 15n38
Transformation, 63, 66n2, 81n54, 94
Trinity, 52, 107–8
Trouillard, J., 16n40, 80n50, 90n94

Union with the One, 78–90
Use and enjoyment, 16, 49, 89, 111

Vergil, 103n55

Wilamowitz, U. von, 86n79

Xenocrates, 36
Xenophon, 84n66, 103n55

Zeno, 30n18
Zeus, 41n4, 42, 83